SPIKE MILLIGAN

MONTY

His Part in My Victory

War Biography Vol. 3

Edited by Jack Hobbs

PENGUIN BOOKS

PENGUIN BOOKS

Published by the Penguin Group
Penguin Books Ltd, 80 Strand, London WC2R ORL, England
Penguin Group (USA) Inc., 375 Hudson Street, New York, New York 10014, USA
Penguin Group (Canada), 90 Eglinton Avenue East, Suite 700, Toronto, Ontario, Canada M4P 2Y3
(a division of Pearson Penguin Canada Inc.)
Penguin Ireland, 25 St Stephen's Green, Dublin 2, Ireland
(a division of Penguin Books Ltd)
Penguin Group (Australia), 250 Camberwell Road,
Camberwell, Victoria 3124, Australia (a division of Pearson Australia Group Pty Ltd)
Penguin Books India Pvt Ltd, 11 Community Centre,
Panchsheel Park, New Delhi – 110 017, India
Penguin Group (NZ), 67 Apollo Drive, Rosedale, Auckland 0632, New Zealand
(a division of Pearson New Zealand Ltd)
Penguin Books (South Africa) (Pty) Ltd, Block D, Rosebank Office Park,
181 Jan Smuts Avenue, Parktown North, Gauteng 2193, South Africa

Penguin Books Ltd, Registered Offices: 80 Strand, London WC2R ORL, England

www.penguin.com

First published by Michael Joseph 1976
Published in Penguin Books 1978
Reissued in this edition 2012

004

Copyright © T. A. Milligan, 1976
All rights reserved

Printed in England by Clays Ltd, St Ives plc

ISBN: 978-0-241-95811-7

www.greenpenguin.co.uk

To Friends of the Earth

Edgington knocks his duff into the fire

Smugglers break the cliff side the fire

Preface

This Volume will cover from the fall of Tunis until our embarkation for the Salerno Landings. I have gone over the ground again, relating in more detail the days preceding the capture of Tunis, using my own diary, those of the Regiment, the Battery, and that of Driver Alf Fildes, who came up with lots of things I'd forgotten, like how much I owed him. During this period, we did nothing but play at soldiers, having good times, having bad times, and times neither good nor bad which consisted of lying in a red hot tent, looking at the join, and pretending you're having a good time, when in fact it was a bad time, but in the main it was a good time. I had with me wonderful comrades who made life worth while, anything that failed was laughed at. It was all a big joke that would stop when Hitler had his chips. Again thanks to Syd Price for his photos, Syd Carter for his watercolours, Mr Bart H. Vanderveen for photos of war time vehicles, Doug Kidgell for committing his memories onto tape, Harry Edgington for his letters, the Imperial War Museum for photographs, Al Fildes for his war diary, and D Battery Reunion Committee for reminding me of many incidents I'd forgotten, like how much I owed them.

393 Orange Grove Rd, Woy Woy, N.S.W., Australia

Editorial acknowledgement

To Mr Moy, a London taxi driver, who returned the manuscript of the book to the editor with no claim for reward and without whom this book would not have appeared.

J.H.

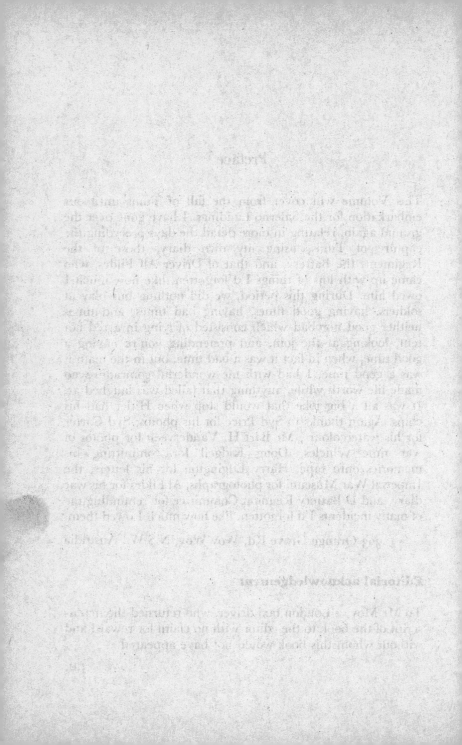

Subject:-Artillery Equipment   141F/2373/11/RA
Comd. 1 A.G.R.A.,   27 June 43
Comd. 2 A.G.R.A.

   I would be grateful if you would congratulate all ranks in 54
and 56 Hy Regts through their Regimental Comds on the
sentence in D.A.D.A., First Army Report dated 22 Jun 43 (in
reply to HQ RA A.F.H.Q. 191/RA of 5 Jun 43) 'The pieces
and recoil systems of howitzers held by units are in very good
order'.
   Knowing how splendidly 7.2″ How detachments performed
in the March–April and May battles, the tribute is well earned.
   The effect of 200 lb shells on enemy morale can be summed
up in one remark by a German officer taken prisoner North of
LONGSTOP 'The fire of your 24 Heavy guns on my
Regiment was quicker and more accurate than any fire
previously experienced by my men'. Only four 7.2″ Hows fired
on this unit. They were manned by personnel of 56 Hy Regt and
fired 800 rounds in 24 hours. The impression appears to have
been indelible.

                    (Sgd)   J.W.L.Pratt Brigadier,
                             Royal Artillery,
                             HQ Force 141

In the Field.
PWHP/VDS.

Copy for:- Comd 54 Hy Regt.,
          Comd 56 Hy Regt.,
          C.C.R.A. 5 Corps (late Comd 1 Hy Regt 1938–1939)

Officers Commanding,   H.Q.14
R.H.C., 15, 17, 18 & 19 Btys 56 Hy Regt. R.A.
   The above copy of letter is forwarded for information.

                      S.N. Rand, Captain, R.A.
                        Adjutant, 56th Heavy Regiment, R.A.
Field.
30 June 43. W.P.

              Copy to Major Chater Jack, R.A.

Our First Victory

May 7th 1943. In a tent, dripping with rain, battery clerk, L/Bdr Mick (I think I'm ruptured) Haymer, rattled a dodgy typewriter and printed 'Tebourba ¾ reported % clear of ½ enemy, @ leading elements of Armoured Div, dntering etc Tunis & ¾.' That day fighting reached maximum intensity, and at 3.20 Tunis fell. 'We got to engage pockets of diehards holding out on Djbel El Aroussia,' said a man claiming to be a Sergeant.

'Wot's die hards?' asked Gnr Birch.

'Well, when you die you go 'ard,' says White, 'like gangsters in cement.'

'That's why they're called hardened criminals,' says Birch.

'You're a cunt,' says Devine.

'Tunis fallen?! Ups a daisy!'

Had we ordinary layabouts beaten the formidable German Army?

'Dear Fuhrer, beaten ve haff been by zer Ordinary Layabouts, signed Formidable German Army.'

'We won,' said White, as though it had been a game of football. Gunner Lee parts his hair, the comb clogged with a six months paté of Brylcreem and dust. 'I bet the victory cost Ladbrokes a fortune, we was 100–1.'

'I hear there's fighting in Cap Bon.'

'You must have good hearing, that's 20 miles away.'

We gathered round the Cook House in a gulley adjacent to the now silent guns. Looming behind us is Longstop Hill, a blood drenched salient taken at Bayonet point by the Argylls. In the twilight our ground sheets glistened with rain.

'What's for the victory feast?' says a cheery voice.

Something that went 'Splush!' was dropped in his mess tin.

MP booking a 17 pounder for parking on the wrong side of the battlefield

May 8th 1943. Deluge. The rain not only fell mainly on the plain in Spain, it also fell mainly on the back of the bloody neck, dripping down the spine into the socks where it came out of the lace-holes in the boots.

Christ!!! we got to move *again*! 'Who runs this bloody

Battery? Carter Paterson?' In darkness we load vehicles. I crash into someone.

'Who's that?'

'Don't know, I think I start with G. Who are you?'

'If this thing on my back isn't a kit bag, I'm Quasimodo.'

I backed a truck down a slope; a scream. 'Owwww fuck!'

'What's that?' I said.

'Me foot.'

'I never knew it swore.' A fist hits me in the earhole.

The move is held up by torrential rain, meanwhile Sgt Dawson has got 'Bludy mulharia' and is taken sweating, farting and shaking to hospital. 'That's what comes of flogging 'is Mepacrin tablets to the wogs as sweets.'

Rain. Mud. Boredom.

'Christ,' said Gnr White, 'I must be bored. I just thought of Catford.'

Occasionally a lorry door would open as an occupant pissed out of the side to cries of 'You're spoiling the carpet.' A creature shining like glycerine approached, his boots great dustbin lids of mud.

'Let me in,' it groaned, 'I can't swim.'

Edgington squeezed in.

'Anything on the wireless?' he said.

'No, the batteries are flat.'

'I thought they were square,' he said.

'I'll turn on the windscreen wipers, it's not much, but it's the best I can do.'

He watched the blades sweep the rain from the glass. 'Ooooohhh,' he groaned in ecstasy. 'What other Army can give you perversions like this.'

The rain is now frightening, the ground is rapidly flooding. 'We better start building a fuckin' Ark' said Sgt Ryan.

Lunch came, lunch went, tea came, tea went, dinner came, dinner went. That was May the 8th 1943. Anybody want to buy it? It's going cheap.

Nazi News Flash

The scene: Mrs Eichmann's boarding house. Bolivia.

HIMMLER: Ach Ein bugger! Ve should never have lost Tunis! If der Fuhrer had only eaten his tin of P.A.D.

GOERING: P.A.D.?

HIMMLER: P.A.D. Prolonged Active Dog. If mine Fuhrer had eaten Prolonged Active Dog, today he would be 159 vid a beautiful coat.

A captured German pilot crapping into the cockpit of his plane in displeasure with the Geneva Convention

May 9th 1943. Dawn. Rain stopped. I prod Edgington.

'Awake! for morning in a bowl of light, has cast the stone that puts the stars to flight.'

'Bollocks.'

'No it was Fitzgerald.'

'Fitzgerald's bollocks then.'

The sun rose, angering the morning sky, and Edgington was none too pleased either.

'Wassertime?' he said, as he unstuck his tongue from the roof of his mouth with a spoon.

'It's hours 0600 darling.'

'It's hours too bloody early "darling".'

He opened his eyes with a sound like the tearing apart of fly papers.

Driver Fildes rapped on the window. 'I'm driving to Tunis.'

Edgington sits up. 'Can I come too?'

'It's about time you came to,' I chuckled. The boot missed me, landed in the mud and sank slowly out of sight.

'It's one legged marching from now on,' I tell him.

We set off across the Goubelat Plain to Tunis, following the wake of the victorious 6th and 7th Armoured. We passed smouldering tanks, dead soldiers in grotesque ballet positions, Arab families emerging from hiding, baffled and frightened, and the children, always the children, more baffled and frightened than the rest.

In the Tunis streets the milling throng are thronging the mills. At a cafe, two German officers drink coffee. Lt Walker asked what they were doing. In perfect broken English they replied, 'Ve are vaiting to be took prisoners old poy.'

We motored slowly through the crowded streets, being kissed several times by pretty girls and once, by a pretty boy.

'No one's kissed me,' complained Gunner Holt, his face like a dog's bum with a hat on.

'Never mind – 'ere comes one now, I'll stamp on her glasses!'

A fat lady with revolving bosoms shouts 'Vive les Americains.'

'She thinks we're Americans,' says Holt.

Some of the beautiful ladies of Tunis greeting our victorious entry

'We'll slip one up her, then blame them,' says Devine.

A group of 'Ities' insist they be taken prisoner or they'll surrender.

'Sorry –' I explain, 'We British Army prisoners.'

The day passed with the drinking of wine and the ogling of women. We were well oiled when two Gunners, The Pills

Our wireless truck 'Fred'

(twins), cadged a lift. 'Either I'm pissed – or he is,' said Devine referring to the twins. The Pills told us the Battery had 'rejoined Regiment on t'other side T'Oued Melah',' by sheer luck we found it in t'dark.

'Have you caught it yet?' greeted Bombardier Dean. He held up a half empty bottle. I recognized the gesture at once.

I must have got pretty stoned. When I awoke next morning I was fully dressed, face downwards, on the roof of a lorry, with a severe attack of face.

'On yer bloody feet,' said a fiend sergeant. We were going into action again!! 'He's bottled up in Cap Bon, so no Tunis tata's today.'

Chater Jack consults his map.

18

'Milligan,' he says, 'we're going into Cap Bon to establish a suitable O P.'

'What's wrong with Lewisham?' I said.

'I've just written home saying – stop worrying, fighting has stopped – now I got to send a telegram saying – Ignore last Letter,' says Driver Shepherd.

'If you want to drive 'em really mad,' I said, 'send a telegram saying – Ignore last Telegram.'

Driver Shepherd has a large boil on his neck covered by a circular plaster. While he slept some artist had drawn a bell push with the word 'press' on it. And they did.

My Diary:

'Motoring inland towards Djbel Ben Oueled. Stop to ask jerry prisoners the way. Chater Jack takes shortest route twix himself and whiskey flask and flags down Mercedes carrying German officers, point blank asks them "Haben ze Schnapps." He gets 3 bottles!'

A message from R H Q. 'Return to base.'

'What!?' said Chater. Snatching the mike, he shouts 'We've only just bloody arrived, who's buggering us around? We've been up since 0600 will you make up your bloody minds, what is the situation . . .'

All was wasted as he forgot to press the transmit button.

'They're all bloody deaf back there. Drive on, Shepherd.' The road is a mixture of Allied and Axis transport, groups of Germans talk with British soldiers. It's all very strange.

'Have you any of that fruit cake left, Milligan?'

'No, sir.'

'Just asking, Milligan. It's a hot evening, I don't see why we shouldn't indulge in a dip, got your costume?'

'No sir, I've learned to swim without it.'

Adjacent to a P O W Camp where a brass band played Tyrolean Waltzes, we enjoyed a delicious swim in the Med. starkers, save Chater who wore his knee length 'drawers cellular', something to do with an officer being 'properly dressed'. The sky turned the colour of a cut throat that bled onto the sea.

British soldier in a sexual trauma brought on by Dorothy Lamour in 'The Road to Morocco'

I swam out about 300 yards then, to my horror, I saw a mine floating towards me. I yelled a warning – 1 part salt water – 2 parts swearing.

Chater Jack shouts 'Quick! explode it with small arms, it's ruining the holiday.' We blazed away, and soon a hundred of His Majesty's soldiers were showing what bloody awful shots they were. Finally, with a roar, the monster exploded.

'*I* hit it!' said Major Chater Jack, 'It was *me*! If anyone contradicts me he'll be on a charge. Now let's get back, it's time for the cooks to poison us.'

On the return journey we pass a village. 'Cretinville!'

'STOP!!!' said Major Chater Jack chuckling; we enter 'Le Hotel Brilliante', a mud hut held together by a door knob and 2 oil lamps. At several tables sat several Arabs drinking coffees. On the wall were posters of Bourguiba. Who?* The Major ordered four Vin Blancs; we repeated the order 3 times, just missing me.

'Let's be getting along, gentlemen,' said the Major.

We followed him into the dark. The truck moved off, and I got the BBC news. 'Axis forces are bottled up in Cap Bon.' If the BBC but knew, we were *all* bottled up. We sang:

> 'We were *drunk* last night,
> We were *drunk* the night before,
> We're going to get drunk tonight
> If we never get drunk any more.
> The more we drink
> The merrier we shall be
> For we are the boys of the Royal Artillery.'

Now *everybody* knew. I picked up a faint German broadcast of a very corny band playing old Jack Hylton arrangements. The singer, could I ever forget his name! – Ernst Strainz! His vibrato sounded like he was driving a tractor over ploughed fields with weights tied to his scrotum.

Back at midnight. The Battery were all wide awake, there were fires, and sing-songs.

'Hello, hello, hello,' said the watchful Edgington, bathing in a tin of hot water.

'Havin' a bath?' I said.

'I found the instruction book.'

Mail! There were letters from parents, a dozen hot knicker girls Arggg!!! and one from Louise!! Argggggggg!!!! Arrrrrrg. Heel. Heel! My parents were well, father was still wearing a wig, brother Desmond was still skinny and being hit by every-

---

* The current President of Tunisia, that's who.

21

one. My father was now a Captain. He re-joined the Army to get the uniform as his own suit had the arse out of it. Since he was a boy, he had been obsessed with the romance of the old West. I grew up with rooms full of guns. He believed that Red Indians lurked in every corner, so all his life he carried a six-shooter. I offer a series of pictures which bear out the story.

Shooting at my mother for breakfast — India 1922

Protective underwear – Burma 1929

23

Fleet Street 1935, about to shoot the Editor of A.P.

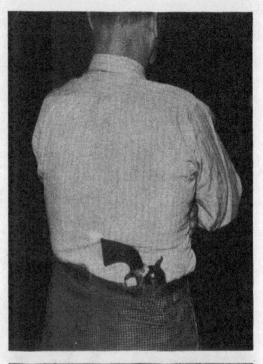

Fleet Street 1935, having killed his editor, now after Lord Beaverbrook

Jock strap to be worn in the shower

Shooting a few wogs before breakfast

25

Killing one of his NCO's for being late on parade – England 1940

I was lucky to have lived through *peace* unwounded.

The letter from Louise left me gasping, I rolled on the ground to beat out the flames.

'What's the matter oh son of khaki?' said Edgington.

'It's the one-eyed trouser snake,' I groaned.

Arggg!! Louise! that night I went to bed, a virile 25 year old Adonis, I awoke next morning a 90 years old, broken-down, onanistic wreck.

May 11th 1943. 'Get up, you dirty little devil,' said a prematurely aged Edgington, breaking his blankets over his knee. May the 11th was exactly the same as the 8th, only worse, much worse, exactly much worse.

Hitlergram No. 091546

The scene: A mixed NAAFI. Tunis.

HITLER: For vy are zer British Tommy Atkins always making mit zer moaning?

TOMMY ATKINS: It's this bleedin' crappy war.

HITLER: How dare you say zat *mein* war is crappy! Zis is zer best var you have had for twenty years! Soon it will be as good as World War One, und *I* vill be in zer Guinness Book of Records! You little Tommy Atkins Creep! Vot did your life consist of pefore eh? Porridge, half pint warm sticky beer, Anton Walbrook in Dangerous Moonlight mit zer bloody awful Varsaw Concerto. Two pounds ten shillings unt one shag a veek! Vid zat vife vid a face like ein chickens arse!

TOMMY ATKINS: You started it all.

HITLER: Me? *You* declared var on *us*! you cock-a-nee creep.

TOMMY ATKINS: That's because you kicked the shit out of the Poles.

HITLER: *Everybody* kicks shit out of zer Poles, zat is what zey are zere for.

May 12 1943. Driver Fildes' War Diary says

'Lazy day at Camp.'
The lads were preparing for visits to Tunis.
'Conquerors! that's what we are,' said Gunner Patrick Devine in thick Liverpudlian tones. A strange Conqueror he looked standing in a tin of hot water, with muscular arms, powerful shoulders, thin white legs and knees that seemed to range up and down his shins when he coughed. Edgington is crouched over Devine's bath, waiting to boil eggs in it.

Swearing (soldiers for the use of) is coming from under a bonnet. 'This truck's had it!' said Fildes. 'When I press the brake pedal the headlights go on and a voice speaks from the steering wheel.'

Sherwood is 'ironing' his K D's, he places them inside two boards, and drives his Bren Carrier on top.

In Chater Jack's tent the telephone rang. 'Hello, CO. 19. Battery. AHHHH!' He put his hand over the mouthpiece.

A repeat performance by Major Chater Jack who made his debut in 'Adolf Hitler: My part in his Downfall'

'It's all over, Von Arnheim has surrendered and he's very angry.'

'This could mean war,' said Lt Budden, who was really in the middle of Beethoven's 5th.

Chater Jack called a general parade. 'It's officially over,' he said with a huge satisfied grin.

'At last we're safe,' said Gunner Forrest, and for the first time in months removed his tin hat. Gunner Woods is puzzled. 'I don't understand, we're fighting *Germany* yet we're in *Africa* bloody miles from Germany.'

'That's because the weather's better 'ere,' says Fildes, 'if you're killed when sun tanned you don't look too bad. Mind you,' he said, 'up North on the Russian front, the cold preserves the body so good, they post 'em back to the relatives.'

May 13th 1943. Bright. sunny. Warm. Breeze: Some Gunners go with Chater Jack to see the results of our counter battery work. A conducted tour of shell holes?? Not for me! We bagged a scout car, Fildes, White, Devine and me (not Edgington, he was kneeling in his tent pointing to it and saying 'Down boy'). We stopped outside Tunis, to dust ourselves, then plunged into the streets; at an outdoor cafe an Iti POW trio played Neapolitan songs, then go round with the hat, 'It's yer own bloody fault for losin',' shouts White.

On this day I met a girl in the street. 'Good morning, would you like me to take you home to have some food?' she said. Food? She took me home to 16 Rue de Lyon, and I met her (wait for it) *family*! 'Vive l'Armèe Premier' they said, which is no substitute for sex. The girl was Daisy Setbon, 17, Jewish-French, about 5 foot 5, olive skinned, with raven shoulder-length hair. She showed us the sights of Tunis; mostly consisting of drunken British soldiers kipping in the gutter.

I wrote to her for 10 years after the war, when suddenly her letters stopped. All inquiries brought no response. Of course! Plunger Bailey! So! the waiting game had paid off.

That evening we were given a dinner at the Setbon's home

as Alf Fildes notes in his diary, *'Had swell meal of spaghetti and beans topped with best red Italian wine.'*

Our truck is missing! We follow a trail of wine and dog ends and find it in the middle of a square; standing in the driver's seat is another square, Gnr White. A truck full of Tunisians were taking it in turns to wear his hat.

𝔖talingram

STALIN: Comrade what kind of a warski is this? Here we are dying by the million and your lot are laying about pissedski in Tunis.

CHURCHILL: You can't stop 'emski. If I report them, their mothers write to their MP's and *they* report me to the Kingski.

Tunis 13 May. The screwing had started. Young Lochinvars, prematurely aged with all night poking, were coming in at first light, paler than the dawn, collapsing on their beds and groaning 'Lovely'. The Great 'Plunger' Bailey decided that degrees of prowess should be recorded. A blackboard was hung on his lorry.

BATTERY SHAGS AS PER MAY 1943

	women involved	number of times	REMARKS
Gunner James	1	6	Tres Bon
Lance/Bdr King	1	1	Brewers Droop
Gunner Forest	1	1	Death through natural causes
Gunner 'Plunger' Bailey	4	20	Resting

Edgington's face darkens. 'How can a man face the woman he loves after all this shagging?'

Said White, 'He could say, "Darlin' I've been keeping in training for you, it's been hard work but worth the sacrifice, for, when it came to my darlin's turn, I'd be fit and ready for her." '

Edgington retaliated, 'You're throwing your love lives away,' he said, lying back in his tent, his socks adrift on his feet, and bent over at the ends. 'Oh no, when I go to the Marriage Bed, I go pure as the driven snow,' which was some statement coming from a long white creature with forearms and knees burnt brown, wearing a vest which just covered his willy, 2 sticking plasters on his inoculated arm, a hair cut that made his head look like a coconut and all of this covered with a fine layer of Tunisian dust. Picture the

A British soldier with an incredible weapon

scene. Suddenly, at the mouth of the tent appears Betty Grable, she sees Edgington. 'Darling,' she says, slowly. He stands up, the pimples on his bare bum showing purple in the half light, he takes her in his arms, and slowly they start to dance out of the tent across the dusty plain in a cloud of dust, his socks slipping off, and the tail of his vest flapping in the breeze.

Letters from Home

13 May 1943. Back home, brother Desmond, filled with post-public patriotism, joined the Air Cadets, he and a gaggle of pimply Freds were given instruction in a cardboard cockpit, *'one of us sits inside, another holds a model of a Stuka, and we shoot it down.'* When my brother's turn came, he would give forth with the entire sound effects of the film 'Hell's Angels', which would end up with him crashing to the ground dying. Then, raising himself on one elbow, he would shout 'Gott Strafe England'. It was all very praiseworthy and a complete waste of bloody time.

My mother took up leather work at night classes. From then on, I received parcels of leather thongs *'in case I needed them'*. Leather gloves with six fingers, leather belts *'in case I needed them'*, a pair of leather garters, leather pay book cover *'to keep it dry'*, leather prayer book cover, then a *'spare leather prayer book cover, in case the first got damaged in the fighting'*. I received the Lord's prayer engraved on a leather medallion – *'it will protect you'*, it didn't. The inside became covered in verdigris and turned my chest green. Were *other* mothers doing this? I didn't see other men in the regiment with green chests wearing initialled leather garters, and gloves with six fingers?

My father was at the R A O C depot, he wore six guns and was teaching his men how to stop paratroops with a *'quick draw'*. His way of stopping Hitler would be to invite him to a game of Poker – then, at a crucial stage, call him *'Ein cheat'*.

He had been a wonderful father, and sometimes, a wonderful mother but kept you on a permanent high. Returning from having seen Richard Dix in 'Cimmaron', he'd kick our

Hitler, having lost at poker to Milligan's father, wondering what he could sell to raise the money

𝕹𝖆𝖟𝖎 𝕹𝖊𝖜𝖘 𝕱𝖑𝖆𝖘𝖍

The scene: the old Bar-Auschwitz.

Two guns blaze – Hitler falls dead – an amazed look on his face – Captain Milligan blows smoke from his guns, S S men step aside in fear, he backs out of the door, there is the sound of screeching brakes as he is knocked over by a dust cart.

front door open, flatten against the wall, and say, 'Cover me while I switch the hall light on.'

I remember watching the spectacular blaze of Crystal Palace from my bedroom window. Father observed it through binoculars, finally he lowered them. 'Navajo!' he said.

My Diary: 14 May 1943. Afternoon to 15 May.

Try to get watches off Iti POW's.
I approached Iti POW.

'You got Tick Tock,' I said and did a superb mime of a watch. He took off his boots. 'No. No – Tick Tock – watch . . .'

I got one for forty stale 'V' cigarettes. They must have killed him within the week; I hope so, the watch didn't work.

We got back to camp late, woke the sentry up and said 'Good night!'

Dear Do
This is a
sample of stuff
propaganda &
heaven a Affrin
under-pvs!!! *****
Loving Bro.
Terry

17th May 1943

AD. Milligan Esq.
1 Linden House
Orchard Way
Reigate
Surrey

'Hi' paratrooper!

May 15th 1943. Off to Tunis again! The Arab drains!!!
'Corrr Christtt,' said Edgington, 'they're worse than
Maunders' feet.'

'True!' I said, 'it takes a thousand years of Arab culture to
build up a pong like this, sniff it all up, tourists pay for this.'

'How do they know which one's theirs,' said Devine
observing women in purdah.

'Easy, outside every wog house there's a weighing machine,
and the husbands just check. "Ah it's darling 16 stone 3 lbs."'

36

'They must have stamina, having twenty wives,' said Devine.

'They don't do 'em all in one go.'

'Ah! but it must be a temptation, I mean, say you have it away with two, you doze off and you wake up at, say, 3 o'clock, you get up for a glass of water and well, it would be silly to go back to sleep when there's another eighteen of 'em crawling up the wall. That's why the men wear those long night shirts in the day time, they got to be ready.'

Approaching are Gunners Musslewhite, Roberts and Wilson, riding donkeys and stoned: days later they were found in Sousse with no recollection of anything. Up before Major Chater Jack, the answer to his question, 'What's your excuse?' was 'Pissed sir'.

'Such honesty cannot go unrewarded,' said Chater Jack, 'case dismissed.'

Oudna

13 May 1943. History of the Regiment says we moved to OUDNA, I won't argue. I was to drive the Major. 'I chose you Milligan because you've never driven me before, and it's time I had another accident.' It was a brief journey.

Oudna was a must for suicides, a barren plain, bisected by a Roman Aqueduct, observing the ruins Gunner Collins remarked, 'Cor, Jerry didn't 'arf bomb that.' He was never commissioned. We arrived in a great cloud of dust which improved the place. Each soldier's features were obliterated. I could, however, tell many by the shape of their boots.

May 15 1943. Edgington was standing outside my bivvy as I lay within. To an observer it would appear he's talking to a tent. As I was asleep, that's exactly what it was.

L/Bdr Trew rushes up. 'Leave is starting!' Great! The band were given from after parade on Friday to Monday mid-day. 'This is more like it,' said Al Fildes, 'wars should be fought like this. We challenge the enemy to a holiday, those who get the best one, win.'

BALFOUR

UNKNOWN JEWISH GUMMER

EDGINGTON

MAUNDERS

NEAT

DEVINE

FORREST

LIDDLE

Boot Recognition Chart

Hitlergram No. 6140823

HITLER: Right! I challenge you! — I will take three months at zer Eagles Nest; Berchtesgarten!

MILLIGAN: A week at Mrs Terrible's Boarding house, Herne Bay.

HITLER: A month at The Schlöss Heidelberg on zer blue Rhine.

MILLIGAN: Ten days at Butlins, Clacton.

HITLER: Three months in zer Grosse Schoener Schoenbrunn Palace, Vienna!

MILLIGAN: 2 nights at the YMCA, Croydon.

HITLER: Six months ... you hear *Six Months* in Gracie Fields Villa, Capri!!!!

MILLIGAN: Checkmate!

HITLER: I don't accept cheques mate, you vill haff to pay cash.

My Diary: 16 May 1943.

Off to Tunis POW camp to scrounge.

We entered the camp. Revenge is sweet, but not fattening. Lt Mostyn's Jewish soul was bent on revenge, he relieved Germans of their watches.

'I'll see that these "gifts" are rewarded,' he said. 'This will get you extra rations,' and handed them a chit declaring, 'This is an anti-Semitic bastard, knock the shit out of him.'

Edgington discovered a Field Kitchen and a Portable Brothel. 'Terrible!' said White, 'the kitchen's full, the brothel's empty.' Rummaging, they found Knäckebrot,* ersatz Kaffee and a selection of German cigarettes.

* Jerry Crispbread.

Hitlergram No. 96133a

HITLER: Mein Gott, zey are smoking our Fags! Zat is terrible.

EVA BRAUN: I know. I've smoked zem.

HITLER: To get our Fags to Tunisia ve had to go through Allied Air Raids on zer Factories! bombs on zer Railways! zer boats to Afrika are torpedoed and zer fags end up being smoked by zat Huddersfield Schit Gunner White!

EVA BRAUN: It's not right and it's not fair.

HITLER: Vot isn't.

EVA BRAUN: Zer left leg of a Joe Louis.

HITLER: I don't vish to know zat, kindly leave zer bunker.

Oudna Idyll

2.20 p.m. I lay in my tent, the heat was terrific, flies and minute dive bombing insects were at large, on the outside of the mosquito net they hung, waiting ... occasionally I displaced them with jets of cigarette smoke. Why should I suffer alone. In the next tent was Gunner White.

'Wot you doin'?' I said.

'I'm laying on me back smokin' a Woodbine with me left hand, and scratching me balls with me right.'

'Say hello while you're there.'

'I was thinkin',' he said, 'at this time back in England on a Saturday afternoon, you know what I'd be doing?'

'No.'

'I'd be in my bedroom, layin' on me bed, smoking a Woodbine with me left hand and scratching me balls etc. Wot'd you be doin'?'

'I'd mow the grass in the garden and my father would sit in a deck chair and encourage me with cries of "It does you good lad", and I'd say to him "why don't you do it then?" and he'd say "Because it doesn't do *me* good, I've tried it".'

'This is a waste of bloody time, my life is going past, time is on the march and here I am on me back in bloody Oudna doing sweet FA. This isn't living! This is ... this is ...' he fumbled for a word, couldn't find it and settled for 'fucking terrible ... what I need in life is variation, something *different!*'

'Right, try smoking with your *right* hand and scratching your balls with your *left*.'

In his tent Edgington starts a tune. 'Lada da da de de' which emerged as 'Red Sails in the Sunset, Way out on the Sea ...' I joined in harmony, this was taken up by Gunner White and in the next tent to Edge, Gunner Tume. One by one the entire tented camp joined in. I got up. I was the only person visible; from the sea of tents the great chorus 'Oh carry my loved-ed oneeee, home safeleeeee to meeee' soared over the sunbaked plain. No one would have believed it. I didn't.

42

British sergeant selling his lorry to an Arab

Oudna: More Letters from Home

A parcel from home! 2/3rds of which are Holy Medals of St Patrick and St Therese. I only need St Andrew and I've got the set, if I had worn every one sent me I'd have weighed 20 stone. Had I died, men searching for my identity disc might have said, 'Christ he *is* St Patrick.' Lt Walker wants to talk to me about the parcel. 'Major Chater Jack has asked me to broach a delicate subject,' he said, 'once in Bexhill, you gave him a slice of your mother's fruit cake which, as you know, he enjoyed full well.'

'That is so sir.'

'Well Milligan, he says that he had mentioned at the time, that if ever you had another cake like it, he was willing to sample a reasonable slice.'

'I don't remember that sir.'

'Well he does. Now, there was a delivery of mail yesterday, and he noticed that one parcel was for you, and on the label it said that among the contents was a fruit cake.'

'That is so sir.'

'He says at Toukebour, you had received a cake, and shared it among the Command Post staff. He said he was on duty at the time, but not actually *in* the command post, and when he heard of the cake he came as quickly as he could but it had all been eaten.'

'I remember that sir.'

'So does he; what I'm coming to Milligan is that he would look on you in a kindly light if you were to give him a slice of the cake which is at this moment in your tent.'

'We've eaten the lot sir.'

'You're a bloody guts Milligan.'

'Yes sir.'

I wrote and told my mother, and lo! she sent him a whole cake, but this never stopped him cadging mine.

'You see,' said Edgington, 'he's just a normal human being like us, he likes his grub.'

'*His* grub?' I said.

We had a morning of morse code training and equipment maintenance. Then came lunch: I ate a slice of 'Spotted Dick' pudding before I realized half the spots were dead flies.

Bombardier Marsden had a lottery. At the end of the day the one who presented most fly corpses won, and it was usually Sanitary Orderly Liddle. How did he do it?

'Look,' he explained, 'when you work with shit, you can't lose.'

We asked him for a percentage, arguing that it was our visits to his establishment which helped to attract the flies.

With the temperature at 100 degrees, I caught the sort of

British tank coming up the road towards a German soldier — a brilliant picture

cold one could only catch on a freezing London night while bathing naked in the Thames.

'Got a cold mate?' says Edgington.

'Yed, I'd god a kode.'

'How did you get that?'

'Badin' naged id der tembes od a freezin nide in London.'

'What's wrong with you now?' says the MO.

'A kode sir.'

'In this weather?'

'Yed.'

'That's like breaking your leg when you're asleep.'

'That's something else I wanted to see you about . . .'

'Come and have a look at this,' says Smudger Smith.

He leads us across the plain to a Cactus grove. There, hidden among the vegetation, is a Stuka, brand spanking new.

'I wonder how much it's worth,' says White.

We swarmed over it, took turns to fiddle with the controls, the engine suddenly gave a tremendous cough.

'What did you do then,' said Smudge.

'I pressed a large red button,' said White.

'For Christ sake don't do it again.'

But White did do it again, didn't he? And the bloody engine started and there we were with this throbbing monster and Pilot Officer White screaming, 'How do you switch the bloody thing off?'

'Don't waste it,' I shouted. 'Bomb the Cookhouse!'

It wouldn't stop, we stood around chucking rocks at the propeller. They bounced off and nearly killed us. It was still ticking over when we were visited by Major Chater Jack. He was furious and kept asking questions, all of which were obliterated by the roar of the engine.

Unable to control himself, Chater Jack drew his Webley pistol, emptied it at the throbbing monster, and drove off.

16 May '43. 'Good morning, Bombardier Milligan,' said Syd Price, fiddling with a camera.

Oudna *Left to right: Gunners White, Milligan, Fildes J Jnr, Fildes Snr. Note Ack-Ack shells bursting overhead*

'What do you want?'

'I wish to take a photograph of the Oudna landscape.'

'There isn't one.'

'I know,' said Price, 'therefore, would you and a few like silly buggers care to pose in the foreground to relieve the monotony?'

The result is the only picture ever taken of Oudna to prove there's no such place. If you are wondering why I'm playing the trumpet, so am I.

'There's a battle scheme starting at 0600 hrs tomorrow.'

We were divided into opposing sides, Ack and Beer – by mid-day thunder flashes kept exploding everywhere, referees would rush up, chalk you with a white cross and say 'you're dead'. I asked Lt Budden permission to throw a thunder flash under our vehicle so that we could play cards.

'Let's have lunch first.' He pointed to a cool conglomerate of date palms.

Halt – in German

A crowd of black faced lunatics jumped us from behind bushes.

'You're all prisoners of Ack Army.'

Says Budden, 'We *are* Ack Army.'

The attackers lowered their rifles, grinned sheepishly and retreated.

'I thought we were Beer Army sir,' I said.

'We don't want *everybody* to know,' said Mr Budden.

A referee roars up. 'You're all casualties,' he said, and marked us with white and red chalk. 'Sign here,' said the referee, 'three dead and two wounded.'

Dutifully Budden signed, the Sgt saluted, mounted his bike, kicked the starter which failed, he kicked again, then several agains, the starter kept sticking, suddenly, when he wasn't ready, it shot back. With a scream he clutched his shin, and well he might, he'd broken it. He lay on the grass, and we radioed up an ambulance.

'Which one is hurt?' said a soppy RAMC orderly.

'I think it's the one on the ground screaming,' said Budden.

As they put him on the stretcher, I marked him with red chalk.

'You bastard,' he said.

We returned to base at the prescribed hour, where dusty and weary, the Battery took tea.

'We must never go to war again,' said Gnr Devine, 'we've lost the knack.'

The great Edgington gave forth: 'Ohhhh,' it says, 'Ohhhhhh,' the sound was from his trembling tent. 'I'm ill. I and my tent are very, very ill.'

He was sweating, steaming, shivering and groaning, a versatile man. He thought me strange for contracting a cold in this climate, now he'd gone one better, he'd got pneumonia. No! he'd gone *two* better, it was *double* pneumonia. We waved as they took him off to dock in a lorry, one man in an empty three tonner, the army were like that. Dutifully we rifled his tent for fags.

GENERAL WAR DIRECTIVE No. 13694

HITLER: Hear zat? one of zer British Army and his tent is ill, let us attack now while zey are under strength!

I decided that we should climb the Roman Aqueduct, so Gunners Forrest, Devine and Milligan set off.

We walked briskly across the dusty flat, the morning young, with a touch of pre-dawn coolness still in the air.

'You never know what you might find at the top,' said Forrest.

The Aqueduct was built of giant stone blocks, no mortar or cement, miraculous. When I tell Forrest and Devine they get the shits, 'It'll fall over,' they said running clear.

'That's it,' I said, 'it's been standing two thousand years and now it's going to fall over.'

We walked around the Aqueduct and came to a low feature. Forrest scrambled up it.

'There, we've climbed it. Let's all go home.'

I was not put off, I led an assault up the ruins till we were a good fifty feet up, close behind, moaning, was Forrest.

'If I wanted to be this high,' he said, 'I'd have joined the air force.'

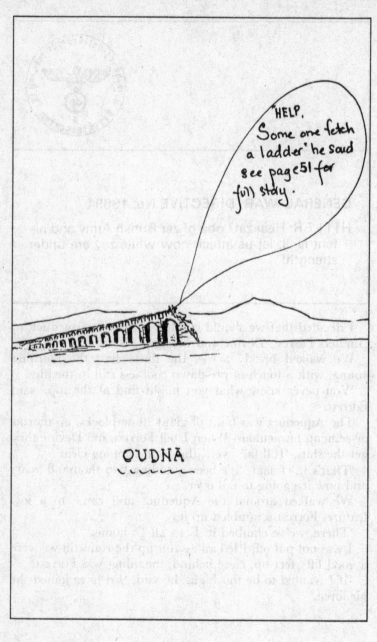

50

'I can't turn round!' said Devine.

'You're not missing anything,' I said.

'It's no good,' said Devine, 'I'm bloody stuck, it's all your fault.'

He was stuck. He stayed stuck for an hour. Despite all my implorings he wouldn't budge. The sun was starting to set and so apparently was Devine.

'For Christ sake,' I pleaded. 'Do something.'

'I think I already have,' he said.

Night was surging across the land. Exasperated, Forrest shouts 'Helppp . . . someone fetch a ladder!'

'A ladder? Round here, you idiot?' I said.

'Alright, clever dick. What else can you shout? "Fetch a 3 piece suite"?'

An American plane flew over.

'Help, fetch a ladder,' I shouted.

Suddenly. Idea!

'Forrest, take yer trousers off,' I said.

'What?'

'Tie 'em together as a rope.'

'I am not wearin' underpants,' says Forrest.

'Living dangerously eh?'

We knotted our trousers together, gradually we managed the descent. Devine's view from underneath must have been something.

'You've got moles on yer balls,' he said.

'A sign of beauty,' says Forrest.

'It is a beauty,' said Devine.

Our descent was being observed by Major Chater Jack, he passed his binoculars to his batman. 'I don't know if my eyes are playing tricks, but there appear to be 3 men climbing the aqueduct with no trousers on.'

'You're right zur – they're not going to do it up there!'

There the adventure ended.

Next morning, Chater Jack said, in passing, 'There's no need to climb that Aqueduct again, Milligan, the water down here is perfectly safe.'

51

Sgt Mick Ryan. No 1 on 'A' Subsection Gun; still wanted by the police

Victory Parade

20th May. 'There's to be a Victory Parade!' Vigorous activity followed the announcement, some of it productive. 'A' subsection gun was chosen for the occasion, men swarmed over the piece, the result was a masterpiece of spit and polish, the 7 point 2 looked beautiful. 'My God, we'll never be able to fire that again,' said Sgt Ryan, 'we'll have to get permission from the Pope.'

May 20 1943. The 'Beauteous Artillery Piece' is limbered

Tunis Victory Parade march past Derbyshire Yeomanry. Our battery's gun in left hand corner. Note 1st Army shield.

General Eisenhower saluting

up and driven under wraps to Tunis. The Parade! Not since
Armistice Day, Poona, had I seen the like; on the saluting
base were Generals galore! Alexander, Eisenhower,
Anderson, Giraud, Admiral Cunningham, Mr Macmillan.

Past the rostrum marched an incredible mixture of soldiers,
Camel Corps, Spahis, Americans, Scots, the Irish, The
Guards, Goumiers, Greeks, Poles, Czechs, Gurkhas, Rajputs,
tanks, armoured cars, in the van came the Free French with
that exciting sound of Bugles and Drums, all followed by a
small black dog. Pity I didn't have a camera. I'd have taken
a picture of myself.

General Eisenhower not saluting

'Order to Move No. 163897639.'

We were to make a new camp on the hills at the back of Hammam Lif, a seaside town just outside Tunis. 'It's a sort of Brighton with camels,' says Tume. Our convoy took us through Tunis and out of the other side, at Hammam Lif we turned off the coast road and climbed the winding back road into the semi wooded hills of Djbel bou Kournime. There, on a plateau, we dispersed the vehicles and made camp. It had been whispered that Jerry indulged in 'drag' activities. Now ... 'What would I do, if I had women's clothes in my big pack, and the enemy were closing in. Put 'em on? No! Bury 'em.' I started to prod the ground, finding a soft surface I dug down and lo! there, just below the surface: One brown dress, one pair of old fashioned bloomers, one padded bra, brown silk stockings. I reported the find to Chater Jack.

MAJOR CHATER JACK:	I can't believe it, Milligan.
MILLIGAN:	It's true sir.
MAJOR CHATER JACK:	You mean they dress up as women?
MILLIGAN:	Someone had to sir.
MAJOR:	I'd heard rumours.
MILLIGAN:	Yes they're very loud sir, on a quiet night you can hear screams.

He handed the 'evidence' over to the Psychological Warfare Department who arrived and questioned *me*. A strange long-haired Corporal with a degree in Psychiatry and BO said, 'Why were you looking for women's clothes?'

I told him it was my day off.

'Do you always look for women's clothes on your day off?'

'Oh yes.'

'Why?'

'It's an inexpensive hobby, with hours of innocent fun. You see, I come from a large family, all girls.'

I could see his programmed psychiatric mind ticking on its predictable way.

'Did you *like* dressing up?'

'I loved it!'

'Have you told anybody else this?'

'My wife.'

'What does your wife do?'

'She's in the Irish Guards.'

He gave me a terrible look and departed. I suppose right now he's sitting behind a desk giving poor bastards tranquillizers and women's underwear.

Hitlergram No. 136

HITLER: Who has been giffing mein Afrika Korps zer drag clothes!

HIMMLER: It vos me meiner Fuhrer.

HITLER: You dumb kopf!! You silly Nana, vy zer poofs do ve have in zer army!

HIMMLER: Nix poofs, zese are drag artists, zey are training to keep up zer morale of zer boys.

HITLER: Vot I hear zer boys have all be up zer drag artists, how can mein Afrika Korps make shoot bang fire fight vit zer sore arses.

HIMMLER: Zey like it mein fuhrer.

HITLER: Like it? Zey must stop it!!! No more zer brown hatting until zer final victory. Give zer order. Stop all zer Browning!

Carthage

22–23–24 May. Our long weekend leave was about to start. Friday till Monday! Where to spend it?

'Edgington,' I said, as I shaved with a thousand year old blade, my face a sea of cuts, 'All my born days I've wanted to see the ruins of Carthage.'

'I think you've only got a pint of blood left,' says Edgington.

'I must hurry.'

'What's a Carthage?' said Doug Kidgell.

'A great archaeological site.'

'Oh?' said Kidgell, 'Why we goin', you got friends there?'

'It's to improve my education.'

'Can't we go to the pictures?' said Kidgell. 'There's Bing Crosby in "The Road to Bali" in Tunis.'

That evening, excited as schoolboys we drove off along the Tunis–Bizerta road, it was as though the war didn't exist, eventually we pull up on a sandy beach for the night.

There was no moon, but the sky was a pin cushion of stars. Great swathes of astral light blinked at us across space. We made a fire, glowing scarlet in cobalt black darkness, showers of popping sparks jettisoning into the night air. Tins of steak and kidney pud were in boiling water, with small bubbles rising to the surface.

'Ready soon,' said Doug, poking the fire, the only poke he would have for a long time.

Fildes and Edgington were making up their beds in the lorry. Edgington singing while Fildes spoke to himself. It was interesting to hear; 'A cigarette that bears lipstick traces – I think I'll put three blankets on top' – 'An air line ticket to romantic places!' – 'It's going to get chilly later' – 'A fairground's painted swings' – 'Better keep my socks on tonight' – 'These foolish things' – 'Where's that bloody pillow?' – 'Remind me of you.'

Kidgell in the driving cab is finishing off an 'I love you for ever' letter.

'You don't write many, Milligan.'

German general repairing Scottish officer's bagpipes under fire.

'I let 'em all worry.'

'What about your folks?'

'Well they worry about me *all* the time. Before the war they worried if I went to the toilet, even if I was in the garden they'd shout out "Are you alright son?" They'd wake me up in the middle of the night and say "Are you alright?" They're natural worriers. My father would wake up at 3 in the morning and worry about his job, and my mother would worry about him worrying about his job.'

'They sound a mite strange mate.'

'A mite? They're insane! Every night, when my father comes home from work, he gets his pistol from under the stairs then shouts "Hitler! if you're in this house, come out with your hands up." Let me tell you, Kidgell, *I'm* bloody worried about *them*.'

We sat around the fire, opening the tins with a Jack knife.

'Army cooks don't like tinned food,' says Kidgell.

'Why not?'

'They can't sod it up in tins. They like fresh stuff they can burn the Jesus out of. The motto of the Army Catering Corps is, Help wipe the smile off a soldier's face.'

'Got him!' said a triumphant Edgington, smashing a mosquito on his wrist, sending his marmalade pudding flying into the fire. 'Bugger,' he said, trying to retrieve it with a stick.

In a food frenzy he dashes to the lorry, returns at speed with rifle and bayonet. A heroic sight, as he lunged time and time again to retrieve the blackened duff. 'Don't forget – thrust – turn – withdraw,' said Kidgell.

'Gentlemen, a surprise!' I produced a small bottle of Schnapps. 'It fell off the back of a Major Chater Jack.'

'That is a spoil of war,' said Edgington, striking a dramatic finger-pointing pose.

'Well, it's not going to spoil mine,' I said, pouring out the white liquid.

Alf sipped and grasped his throat. 'Christ! If they drink this, they *are* the master race.'

It was fiery stuff.

'It'll kill us,' said Edgington.

He spat a mouthful on the fire, it exploded in a sheet of flame. 'See? When you go to the bog, for Christ's sake don't strike a match.' We mellowed. Harry got hiccups.

Edg: I wonder – hic – what's going to hickhappen to – us
next –'

He didn't have long to wait for the answer – a spark shot out of the fire and burnt him.

We sat close to the fire. The smoke kept the mossies away – an occasional brave one would die under hand as it landed.

'Silly sods. I wouldn't risk my life to pass on malaria,' said Fildes. 'I think I'll turn in.'

Through the night a 3 ton lorry, with a mosquito net across the back, was home to four lads from London, who slept sounder and safer than those *in* bomb ridden London. It seemed all wrong, but it was alright by me.

Scottish soldiers surrendering their underwear to the enemy

A letter told of my eccentric father's career as a Captain. He had decided that the RAOC Depot at Reigate was wide open to paratroops. He took it upon himself to make a life-like raid on the Depot. He briefed a dozen NCO's. They chose mid-day. The officers are in the Mess, having a pre-lunch pissup – the men are queueing in the mess hall. Suddenly the cookhouse staff are surrounded by men with black faces and tommy guns. Their leader is speaking in a strange patois. ''Ands up, Schnell, git against that bleedin' wall, Englander please.' In the Officers Mess from behind the bar arose 5 men with blackened faces, one wearing a German helmet, and holding a machine pistol, 'Last orders pliss undt hands up.' It was my father. The officers were then locked in an office where it was simple to phone police. A constable arrived, and my father then explained the whole scheme. The Colonel said:

'You're a bloody fool,' and had him posted to RAOC, Elstree.

We were up at first light and away through Tunis on the Carthage road.

'Let's play some party games,' I said, 'I make up the first line and you have to rhyme the next, "There was a young gunner called Harry" '

KIDGELL: Told the MO he wanted to marry,
EDG: The MO said Oh?
ALF: Is it Bexhill Flo?
ME: He said No, it's old Calcutta Carrie.

The blue Mediterranean flanked the road, we were as free as we would ever be in our lives. We pulled up at a lonely beach, plunged into the azure waters, with Edgington as base man we repeatedly tried balancing on each other. We got as far as 3, then collapsed with great artificial screams and dramatic plunges into the briny. One of us would submerge and sing a song and from the rising bubbles you had to guess what tune it was. Life was golden, and we were the assayers. Evening; we made camp by a sandy verge. We ate and talked. At 9.30 we bedded down. 'Good nights' were exchanged. At midnight we were still talking.

'This is marvellous, isn't it?' says Edgington, 'I don't like going to sleep 'cause I'll miss it.'

DOUG: Holidays in Africa, cor.
EDGE: You gone quiet Al!
AL: I was thinking of Lily.
ME: You dirty little devil, sleep with your hands on top of the blankets.
AL: You don't know what true love is Milligan, there's too many birds in your life.
ME: I spread my investments! Keep as many on the boil as you can, I've got 7 going for me back in England, see there's –
EDGE: Look out! He's going to have a roll call!
ME: There's Beryl – Marie – Kay – Ivy – Madge – Betty – Dot – Doris.
DOUG: Companyyy! stand at easeeee!
AL: Don't they ever find out about each other?
ME: I keep the door locked.
EDGE: You're evil Milligan, with all that shaggin' it's going to drop off one day.
DOUG: Believe me, it won't half make a noise when it hits the ground.

We awoke at first light, and played 'Who's-going-to-make-the-tea?' By ten past 9 no-one had given in, finally Edge arises, bent double, bladder bursting. 'I'll make it.' 'He'll only *just* make it,' I thought.

We heard him tinkering about outside, he broke into a little tune.

> Don't blame me,
> For falling in love with you.
> I'm under your spell
> But how can I help it don't blame – *BUGGER!*

'How's he going to rhyme that,' I thought. He'd burnt himself. With Edgington, striking a match could lead to anything. Edgington tying a boot-lace could end up with a broken arm. Edgington cutting his toe nails could mean an amputated leg.

'Come and get it!'

We got it, fried eggs and sand. It was just after 10 a.m. when Doug put the lorry in gear and started following the signs.

'What happened at the Carthage?' said Doug, who was still puzzled.

A British soldier forcing an Arab to smash his foot with a large hammer so as to effect an early discharge

'It was a great Naval Power! Had a war with Rome, I forget the score. The Romans razed the city, and ploughed the ground with salt.'

'How did you know all that?'

'Chambers Encyclopaedia,' I said, 'as a kid I loved reading. Given a chance I could have been a great scholar, even University.'

'You could have been a great University?'

'Everyone ought to get a university education,' said Al. 'I reckon if Harry had been through a university, he might be writing concertos instead of burning himself makin' the tea.'

'I think he'd burn himself writing a concerto.'

'Chambers Encyclopaedia?' said Harry. 'I thought that was the history of Piss Pots.'

Without warning, Kidgell burst into song. 'Loveeeeeeee let me taste the wine from your lipssss,' and then went into hysterical laughter.

'He's goin' off his nut,' said Edgington, 'it happens to short arses like him.'

Doug frowned, smiled and grimaced as only a facial cripple could. 'Short arsed men are well known for their power. Take Nelson.'

'You're not,' said Fildes querulously, 'you're not lumping yourself in his class?'

A smile played across Kidgell's face.

'Answer, answer,' shouted Edgington, banging his fist on the dashboard and cutting his finger.

'Yes,' said Kidgell, 'I do, I have the same short arsed qualifications as 'im, it's just that I never had the same chances.'

Al turned and looked at Kidgell.

'What are you staring at?' he giggled.

'Christ,' chuckled Al, '*you* in charge of the H.M.S. Victory?'

'How do you know that inside me there isn't a brilliant naval tactician?'

'Say Ahhhh,' I said, 'and I'll look for him.'

'Personally you look more like a $\frac{1}{2}$ Nelson,' said Edgington.

'Alright, alright, you think what you want, I still say short

65

arses have a greater power over their fellow men by reason that they're nearer the ground and haven't got so far to fall.'

That baffled the lot of us and we gave up. Edgington was bending his fingers over each other to make 'Crab Claws'. 'I learned this as a nipper,' he said. We set off again, sucking our ration of boiled sweets.

We were doing 15 miles an hour, at that speed you could say 'Look at that', but, at modern speeds it's 'Did you see that?' Finally, CARTHAGE! We parked by a clump of trees, and walked to the ruins of the amphitheatre.

It was almost featureless now. What a sight it must have presented, clad in marble, as high as El Djem, the sun of Africa reflecting its white surface, the roar of crowds, the blood, the mangled remains, like Celtic vs Rangers.

'Is this it?' said Doug.

'Yes.'

'*This* is what I missed Bing Crosby on the Road to Bali for? It's terrible, it's like Catford.'

'One minute you're allying yourself with Nelson and when

A postcard I sent home at the time. It shows the amphitheatre at Carthage that Kidgell objected to

you see history you say it's Catford! You short arse, I only brought you here because the ruins were low enough for you to see over.'

'Well,' says Kidgell, 'I still say a Carthage is not as good as Bing Crosby in the Road to Bali.'

We brewed our tea on the floor of the arena, it was hard to believe blood spilled here 2,000 years ago.

We upped anchors and drove on, finally Doug picked a spot adjacent to a heavily bombed French maritime repair docks.

'Ah!' says Kidgell, 'This looks more like a Carthage.'

He backed the truck under a large tree – a small group of Arabs with 3 donkeys and a camel are passing towards Tunis. They sell us oranges, eggs, dates and things that look and taste like Pistachio nuts, mainly because they were.

After a day of swimming, we are in bed smoking and talking.

'Got to be back by mid-day tomorrow – sod it,' said Doug regretfully.

'Good night lads,' yawned Edgington.

'Steady,' I said. 'You haven't had an accident for an hour.'

Back to the Battery

We arrived back dead on time, 6 hrs late. What's *this*??? *Move* at dawn???

'Where to?'

'Somewhere else,' we were told.

'We're already somewhere else,' I said.

'This bloody moving,' said White, 'I should write to my MP.'

'Why don't you?'

'He's a cunt, that's why; he's in the Navy – 2nd Class stoker.'

'If you voted him in you're all cunts.'

'No, we're not, huddersfield is a very intelligent town.'

'Then why did you say it with a small h?'

67

Men of the 7th Batt. Black Watch, almost out of their minds with boredeom, recreate a Busby Berkeley musical happening

'Pardon?'

'Huddersfield? They're at the bottom of the third division!'

'Because all their players are in the Kate.* You know how old the current goalie is?'

'No.'

'68. He had 13 own goals and two heart attacks last season.'

Move from Hammam Lif

My Diary. May 27 '43. We leave Hammam Lif and move to destination 'Secret'.

'Secret?' said White, 'Soon there'll be 6 bloody Regiments there, how do you keep that lot quiet?'

* Kate: Kate Carney = Army.

'If we was tourists, how much would this trip cost us?' said Edgington.

'Thousands,' said White.

'Ah yes,' said Gunner Maunders, 'but this is travelling 3rd Class.'

He was speaking from an agonized position atop reels of signal wire; sans boots and socks, with his feet reeking in the heat.

White was stretched on a pile of blankets, most of which were in better nick than him, he was about to light the briefest of dog-ends. I pondered on how he could do it without scorching his nose; he produced a piece of cardboard which he slipped under his nostrils, as a kind of fire guard.

'Neccitas et mater inventum,' said the learned Bombardier Deans.

'What's that mean?' said White.

'It means, Gunner White doesn't speak Latin.'

'Who needs Latin?'

'It's a dead language,' chips in Edgington.

'But he's just spoke it, and he's not dead.'

'He learnt it for when he is,' I said.

Lunch. In the shade of the olive trees we sat and ate our sandwiches, and then drove on. Life was timeless.

Deans was running through a 'Filmgoer' 1 year old. 'Clark Gable has joined up. He's an air gunner,' he said.

'That's not a very big part.'

'The war has been badly cast,' I said. '*I* should be playing the part of a rich conscientious objector living with Joan Blondell who has to be massaged, nude, every hour with hot chocolate.'

Posters on trees are calling on the French to join the 'Armée Libre Française'.

'Bloody fools,' said Maunders. 'I wouldn't join up because of a poster.'

'Haven't you ever 'eard of Patriotism?' said Deans. 'Suppose Jerry invaded England – and tried to screw your sister. Wot would you do?'

'I couldn't do nothin' could I? I'm in bloody North Africa.'

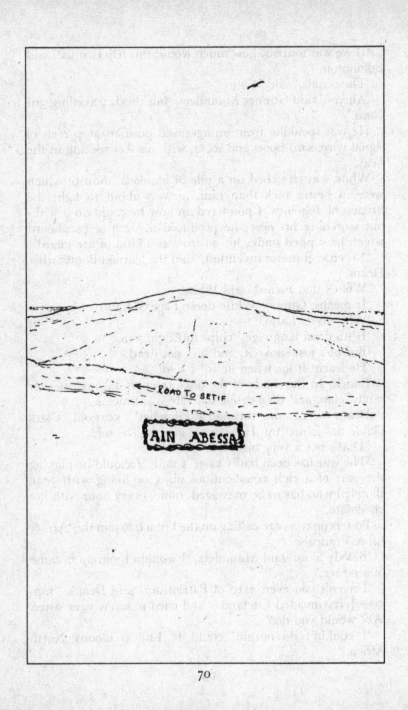

May 30/31 1943–1st June. 'We're here,' said someone. 'We're here' was a place called Ain Abessa. We all leapt enthusiastically from our lorries to be confronted by another desolate plain with a slight rise in the middle.

'That rise, gentlemen,' said Lt Budden, 'is home.'

The heat was stifling, even the crows were walking.

'I saw Ronald Colman in Beau Geste and he never sweated like this,' said Bombardier Fuller.

'Perhaps they shot it in Norway,' I said.

My father had told me 'there's always more breeze on a slope', I leaned to the left but felt no cooler. Evening came. I filled my water bottle for the night, and took Mepacrin. I couldn't sleep. Why was there a war? Could it have been avoided? Why didn't *I* avoid it? By now I could have been making my way as a trumpet player through the ranks of the big bands. Perhaps one day I would play with Tommy Dorsey and screw Helen Forrest. By dawn's early light I wasn't in Tommy Dorsey's Band, and the only screw was holding up the tent pole.

The cookhouse waggon was missing, 'I don't miss it at all,' said White. We ate the remains of yesterday's haversack rations which now looked like an operation.

After Parade, we spent all day putting Signal gear into a Nissen hut, and testing the equipment.

By mid-day, the cooks had arrived! We stood in the broiling sun, watching the sweating cooks as they ladled out Maconochies and rice pudding. We retired to our tents to escape the flies.

My bivvy was roomy, I had increased its height by adding a three foot purple canvas wall along the trailing edge and dug down three feet so that I had more head room. An electric light ran from the truck, there was a wireless set by the bed and the fridge was on order. Over the roof I had put a fly sheet making the tent some ten degrees cooler.

One afternoon Edgington and I were practising post-war sleeping, when the distant voice of L/Bdr Sherwood was heard. 'Oi, you in there.'

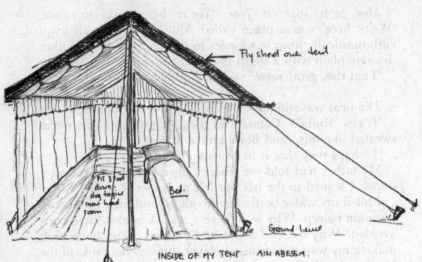

Fly sheet over tent

Pit 3 feet down: dug to give more head room

Bed.

Ground level

INSIDE OF MY TENT: AIN ABESSA

'Hello?' (me)
'I bet you I can get you out of that tent in minutes 2.'
'Balls –'
'10 francs.'
'Done.'
'Right – minutes 2 starting *now*.'
We doze on.
'Minutes 1 and 40 secs,' shouts Sherwood.
I hear a combustion engine approaching. I have a nasty feeling: I raise the tent flap. A Bren Carrier is nearly upon us. The bastard! He'd put it in bottom gear, pointed it at our tent and let it loose unmanned!
'Fuck! He's going to win,' says Edgington.
'No, he's not, grab that tent pole, I'll take this one.'
'That was cheating,' said Sherwood as he unscrews his wallet. He had to run 400 yards after the Bren and we had to reset up our tent. All for 10 francs. We were bloody mad.
The Arabs had rifled the tombs of the Pharaohs, now it was our turn. Chalky White was asleep. A brown hand came under the tent flap, White hit it with a pick handle, and there was an agonized, 'Ow fuckin' 'ell.' It was Gunner Devine feeling for White's fags.

Kerrata Gorge. Holiday

2nd June 1943. Chater Jack realized Ain Abessa was lowering morale, so again he set up more holidays. With Lt Budden and Sgt Dawson in charge, Gunners Edgington, Fildes, Shipman, Tume, Carter, Bdr Deans and Milligan drove to the Kerrata Gorge. Through tortuous mountain roads we drove amid a magnificent wild scenery.

The road had been hewn from solid granite, and on the floor of the gorge was a giant engraved stone 'Le Travail du Militaire Française 1882'. It was a masterpiece of construction. Gradually through a series of tunnels, the road descended to the floor of the gorge level with the river Agrioun; adjacent was perfect ground for camping. We pitched our Iti 10 man tent under a tree, facing the river! The back drop to all this was the great Kabylie range of mountains. Soon the quiet of the gorge was broken by shouts and splashing. The walls of the gorge rose three hundred feet, and, growing in abundance by the stream were pink and scarlet

Kerrata Gorge, North Africa

River   we camped here

Rhododendrons. With towels wrapped around our middles we sat in the shade, Al Fildes strummed 'Come with me, to Blue Hawaii'. 'Pity we can't share this with the poor buggers from home,' he said.

'We *are* the poor buggers from home,' I reminded him.

Lt Cecil Budden swims without his specs, colliding with rocks, cliffs and driftwood and comes out a mass of bruises. I can see him now with those magnificent PT shorts hanging below the knee like wet concertinas. Edgington! now *there* was style, again those draggley drawers, the cheeks of his bottom peek-a-booing above the elastic, he was somewhere in the Tarzan/Gregory Peck mould. His approach to the dive was to make a fifty yard momentous run-up, reach the water, trip and fall face in. As he surfaced (usually upside down) he put on that 'man of Action-Sport-and-Labour Exchange'-look, and then, with an over-arm stroke, he would set off, a look of determination on his fine face.

Edgington 'surfacing'.

Gradually he would sink from sight, the only man in the world who had learnt to swim downwards.

There was no organization, someone cooked one day, someone else another; it worked out very fairly, especially for me. I did bugger all.

Climbing Kerrata Gorge

3 June 1943. It was first light, a cool morning, with the sound of the river singing in the dawn. 'Hands off cocks – on with socks,' said a voice.

As we unravelled ourselves from the blankets there was the usual 'Anybody-seen-my-boots/socks/teeth/trousers/etc/?' It seemed like every night a giant spoon came and stirred the whole contents of the tent into a cloth porridge.

'Wot's for breakfast?' Al Fildes pointed to something in the pan. 'It's brown and black but tastes green!'

'Is it an omelette?' I said.

'That is the current opinion,' said Lt Budden.

So then it was up the gorge. It was tiring but not dangerous, but to *Edgington*! that *was* dangerous! We crossed the road to the West wall where a clear water stream was falling from above. I suggested that we follow it. I said, 'Look, there is a clear water stream falling from above. I suggest we follow it.' We started to ascend, grabbing tufts of grass, bushes, roots and each other. At a hundred feet we paused on a small plateau where a pool had formed, scuttling about in its depths were fresh water shrimps.

'Cor,' says Tume, 'how did they get up here?'

'They climbed up the water,' I said.

The morning was gradually going from warm to hot, and we went with it. At about two hundred feet it became a bit precipitous, people were saying 'Whose silly idea was this?' 'We should be roped together,' said Edgington, whose position appeared to consist of one foot *above* his head on a ledge, and his other one dangling in space. Indeed Edgington *should* have been roped together.

We had reached three hundred feet, the top seemed no nearer. 'Someone keeps addin' a bit on,' explained Dean.

A brief description of the flora, among trees I saw Portuguese and Afare's oak, elm, ash. The shrubbery round about was a mixture of strawberry tree, Myrtle and woody climbers such as clematis. They were in various stages of flower and gave off a beautiful perfume at night, which was usually lost in clouds of tobacco smoke.

'I can smell a dinner,' said Edgington, now in the shape of a swastika. 'Look!'

He pointed down to the camp way below where Fildes was stirring a large pot. The mention of *food* is fatal, immediately the massed legs started downwards like homing pigeons.

We all drew nigh to Al Fildes with sharp appetites. 'What's cooking then?' we asked. 'It's my laundry,' he said, whereupon we taketh Edgington, and throweth him in the river. Budden came forth to see a soldier swimming fully clothed.

'What are you doing man?' he asked.

'I'm teaching my battle dress to swim sir.'

June 5th. Friday 1943. 'There's wild pigs, up the mountain,' the information was imparted by one Mahmoud, an Arab who came scrounging fags and whose head was therefore a mass of lumps; he would act as our guide if we wished. A pig for dinner? Marvellous, none of us were Jewish. Al Fildes' diary reads: '*Sgt Dawson and party set off with rifles and ammo, have dug 3 graves.*'

We left at 1900 hrs and were taken up a mountain path that brought us to a plateau, we arrived as the light faded. We climbed a tree and waited. Midnight. All fags gone. We were losing hope. Suddenly, Mahmoud let off a terrifying Arab fart. 'Christ!' said Jordy Dawson. 'No wonder the Crusaders lost.' I fell out of the tree laughing, the hunt was over. We trudged back to the camp fire, Bombardier Dean was sharpening a carving knife – 'You tell 'im Sarge; you're biggest.' Deans took the news well and tried to commiserate saying 'You're a lot of cunts – we could have gone to bed' whereupon Gunner Edgington accidentally looses off a round that nearly parts Bombardier Deans' hair. 'That bloody does it,' said Deans.

Bdr Deans clutching himself through his pocket

The night was saved from complete disaster by things called Sausages.

We ate in silence. 'Pass the wine,' said Edge who, himself, has been passing wine for months. Sgt Dawson was occupied with a whisky bottle, trying to wean himself off food.

'After the war, I'm going back to my old job,' said Gunner Shipman.

'What old job?'

'Any old fucking job . . . .'

Finally at about three in the morning the chilly night air drove us to our beds. An unforgettable day.

Last Day at Kerrata

June 6th 1943. My Diary: Last day: We swam at first light, and wished we hadn't. It was bloody cold. Edgington was cringing in the water, his teeth chattering, singing his latest hit:

It's chilly,
On yer willy,
In the water
In Kerrata.

'Rubbish,' I said.

'Rubbish? If Cole Porter was writing this stuff they'd be lapping it up, it's only my words against his.'

Why we should go mineral rock hunting escaped me. We searched the area.

'What's a fossil?'

'The birth mark of a dead animal.'

'There must be gold around here.'

Soon our pockets were bulging, we would ask Budden's advice, after all *he* was a university man, an officer, not only that he was also intelligent. When we arrived back he was not only a University man, an officer and intelligent, but dead asleep with his mouth open.

'Don't wake him,' I said, 'he might be dreaming of promotion.'

We carefully sorted the rock samples into the various categories that we knew – big and small.

General Anderson and senior officers wondering what to do now the Campaign is over

It was gone 3 when Budden arose, such was his condition that his first words were, 'We must be ready by mid-day.'

We showed him the samples. 'They're rocks,' he said, we told him we knew that, and he said so did he.

'Aren't they *valuable* sir?' I said.

'I don't know,' he replied.

What a fine officer I thought, he could have lied and said 'Yes, they are gold bearing of a high degree,' but no! he had fought back the temptation and deprived us of a fortune! We had final swims, and then set off to Ain Abessa.

EXTRACT FROM BATTERY ORDERS
by
MAJOR F. CHATER JACK, D.S.O., M.C., R.A.

COMMANDING 19/56 HEAVY REGT, R.A.

FIELD.   11.6.43

---

1. INFORMATION.

The Battery will be interested to learn that they hold the record for the greatest number of 7.2" rounds per gun fired in 24 hours.

The figure is 220 on 23rd April '43 and these, as will be remembered, were on the targets involved in the fight for 'LONGSTOP': the Battery positions being then at TOUKABEUR.

The next highest figure is 134 r.p.g. fired by two other Btys of 56 Heavy Regt, during the final attack on 6th May '43 when the two Arm. Divs broke through to TUNIS and the Peninsula.

Third comes a figure of 80 r.p.g. also fired by 19 Bty on 24th Apl '43 during the final assault on and capture of 'LONGSTOP'.

During the final battle of MEDJERDA Valley between 22nd April and 6th May, 19 Bty fired a total of 2340 rounds the next highest of any 7.2" Bty being 1564.

F. Chater Jack
Major, R.A.

FIELD.   COMMANDING 19/56 HEAVY REGT, R.A.
11.6.43
AGP

79

'2340 rounds? No wonder we were shagged out.'

12 June 1943. Sgt Dawson and his pissy friends had spent all night at a cafe in Kerrata village on the booze. They arrived back at dawn, awoke me with a mug of tea loaded with whiskey, and, half awake I downed the lot; in ten minutes I was raving drunk, and had to be held down by Smudger Smith and 3 Gunners. Hitting me lightly with rifle butts, they carried me screaming to a distant tent.

'What's all that shouting coming from the direction of Algiers?' said Major Chater Jack.

'It's Bombardier Milligan sir,' said Dawson. 'He's running through some ideas for the band sir.'

'You sure he hasn't caught them in a rat trap.'

'No sir – they're outsize.'

Sgt Donaidson

80

Wed. 9th June 1943. Sitting outside his tent, swigging warm beer Sgt Frank Donaldson tells me the truth about the 'battle' at the El Aroussa Wagon Lines on Feb. 26/27. One morning, a large cloud of dust disappeared through the Wagon Lines, 'What was that?' said Donaldson.

'Our Front Line,' was the reply. They received an order: 'Fuck off as quick as you can,' but! BQMS Courtney told Donaldson, 'Stay behind to defend the road.'

'There isn't one,' said Donaldson.

'That's not my fault,' said Courtney and departed. Donaldson and Co. noticed a stew simmering for lunch, they were about to partake when the convoy roared back again, snatched up the stew and disappeared yet a second time.

A Lieutenant wearing a ragged green beret arrived on a

The Afrika Korps having lost North Africa try to play their way back to favour with the Fuhrer

lady's bicycle, and said he was from the Reconnaissance Corps. He suggested they climb a hill to see what the noise on the other side was. 'They saw it, and to a man they shit themselves.' There, forming up, were massed German Infantry and Tiger Tanks.* There was a hasty retreat to the foot of the hill. The Lt ordered everyone to stay put, and then buggered off. They heard tanks approaching, and there was further stomach trouble. Gnr Forrest pointed to a pile of rocks and abandoned pick handles.

'We'll need them,' said Forrest.

'Wot for?' said Donaldson.

Said Forrest, 'When tanks come, we chuck rocks at turret, and when bloke inside opens turret to see what noise is, we hit him on the head with pick handle . . .'

I could hear the screams of 'Kamerad!' as the vicious pick handles bit deep into the four inch armour plate.

Lucky for Donaldson, Churchill Tanks of the North Irish Horse came on the scene and saved them for a worse fate – cold stew for dinner.

Chater Jack had cheerfully told the Mayor of Setif that he had 'une belle Orchestra de Jazz' so we found ourselves playing at 'Thé Dansant', where 500 Gunners tried to dance with 2 girls and an old French matron, with a face like Schnozzle Durante's pulled inside out. The place, I recall, was the Salle de Fête. Edgington called it a Fête worse than death.

As I lay abed that night a voice was heard singing

'No rose in all the world,
Until you came . . .'

It was full of tender meaning, the voice floated on the night air, in the silence of the giant Continent it seemed strange to hear that voice – a young English voice. The song continued and soared until it concluded on a high exquisite delicate falsetto. Silence settled on the land.

* He was mistaken, they were Mark IIIs.

'Thank fuck, 'e's finished,' said a voice. It was one of those little cameos that lightened the darkness.

French Concert Party

Fri. 18th June 1943. 'Milligan? Band is to report to 74 Mediums, music playing, for the uses of.'

At 74 Mediums camp we were greeted by a humptey-backed Captain who appeared to be training for death.

'I'd like you to do your turn in the miggle of the show.'

'When?'

'The miggle of the show.' He definitely said mi*gg*le – so! he couldn't pronounce his D's. 'How woulg you like to be announceg?'

I paused. 'D Battery Dance Duo and Doug on Drums.'

Carefully he wrote it down.

Would we like drinks? OK. The stage consists of trestle tables covered with blankets. I am a trumpet player covered in battledress. A charabanc arrived with the Algiers Opera Company. First to alight was Soprano Mlle Beth Villion, she must have been 15 stone, the charabanc rose 3 ft when she got off. 'Cor,' said Harry, 'there's enough for all of us.' She was followed by a petite soprano, Mlle Garcia. 'You're mine, all mine,' says Doug clutching his parts, next came a crazed mop-headed French Algerian Pianist.

A tent had been erected for the ladies to change in. Gunner Liddle detected a hole in it . . . what he saw set his testicles revolving, Mlle Villion was sitting on a stool, naked, making up; Liddle a sporting man, spread the word. My god! the size! She could sit in one spot and still be several other places at the same time.

The concert started, and finally it was our turn. The Captain announced 'I have great pleasure in announcing G Gattery Gance plus Goug on Grums.' Got 'im! We belted through our numbers, got a great reception, and then cleared for Mlle Garcia. During the interval a human being dressed up as a Gunner approached me. 'You don't know me from Adam,' he said. I told him he must be better dressed.

The stranger was Gunner Snashall (Snatch) from the 8th Survey Regiment, he said he played the violin and could he sit in on the next session. OK, we said. It turned out that he was great, a real good Jazz violin player, though the fact that he appeared with a garland of wild flowers around his head was a bit disconcerting.

Gunner Snashall

Setif – Musicians resting!

Mlle Villion in a black silk dress was approaching, her bosoms going on ahead of her by ten seconds.

'You play zee jazz verre good, you naughty boy,' she said.

'Help! massage,' I said weakly.

We listened spell bound as she sang the Habanera from Carmen, her voice was pure silver. In the warm African night, it was an unforgettable experience, with the moon shining down on those lovely white boobs. She stopped the show, but then she was big enough to stop anything. The show over we waved the French artiste and her boobs good-bye. A letter from Snashall reminds me how the evening concluded, 'I remember the French Ensa charabanc disappearing into the night, then afterwards, Harry, Al, Doug and I in the back of a 3 tonner with a quarter moon, palm trees, you on guitar playing and us singing, Come Rain . . . Come Shine . . .'

Birth of the 2 Agra Concert Party

19 June '43. Part two orders: 'It has been decided to form a Concert Party. Anyone who has the ability to entertain will parade tomorrow at 1000 hrs, MAP REFERENCE 345 675.' This turned out to be a deserted field and a tree.

At ten o'clock trucks with the 'Artistes' appeared, the 'Judges' were Captain Graham Leahmann, L/Bdr Ken

Captain Graham Leahmann

Carter * and a Regimental Padre who shall remain anonymous. A man would step forward, click his heels, and say 'Hi will now sing "Honley a Rose" ', burst into song, finish and salute. It must have puzzled, nay, baffled the Arabs; for what possible reason was that English Infidel doing a vigorous soft shoe shuffle in the middle of a field, gradually disappearing in a cloud of dust, finally coming to attention and saluting two men standing under a tree.

I'd seen many army auditions, I recall one at Hailsham. A crowd of soldiers had turned up 'To find the Stardom'. It's a fact that an idiot doesn't know he's an idiot, he may think he's a great singer or dancer. The auditioning officer said, 'First one please.' A squat Scot with a terrible squint and a Glaswegian accent stepped forward. 'Rifleman MacToley.'

'What do you do.'

'I'm a musician, sir.'

'What do you play?'

'The spunes, sir.'

'What?'

'Spunes, like you eat yer dinna wi'.'

'Ah, yes. Do you have any music?'

'I canna read music, surr, I'm naturally gifted.'

Producing two spoons he started, 'Ah should lak tae pay my tribute tae the late George Gershwin, by whistlin' Rhapsody in Blune.' It was appalling! It had nothing to do with Rhapsody in Blue, he frequently dropped the spoons, with a cry of 'Whoops, sorry sir' and would then start all over again.

The auditions continued with soldiers who thought the world could be entertained by the walking on hands, the doing of cartwheels, press ups, somersaults and the standing on the head.

One idiot's act consisted solely of falling flat on his back. 'Is that all?' said the officer. 'Yes sir, it takes it out of you.' 'Well take it out of here,' was the reply, but from the Auditions at map reference 345 675, in N. Africa came the best British Soldier Show of the war.

* Now Producer of 'Crossroads'.

21st June 1943. It was a great day for Al Fildes. He won 195 francs on Nasrullah in the Derby. He felt good, and decided to buy the lads drinks. It cost him 200 francs.

22 June 1943. Ziama was a bay on the coast of North Africa. It was as unspoilt as at the beginning of time, so, the Army decided to fuck it up, and build a NAAFI and Rest Camp there. The beach was copper coloured, sunlight reflecting from the bottom gave the water a shimmering Caesar's royal purple colour. Behind us were scrub covered hills, with Acacia trees where occasional troops of Barbary Apes could be seen, their little black faces peering down on their less fortunate brethren.

We had enjoyed a day of peace, sunshine and NAAFI. In the evening, without any warning – comes a cloud of red dust – travelling at 100 mph – it tries to blow the camp into the Med – but we find safety inside the lorries. We watch as tents are wrenched from the ground and blown out to sea, revealing the startled occupants still in bed. Staff wrestled to hold down the NAAFI marquee, flapping, like a giant eagle about to take off – a stream of cups, saucers, spoons and buns, shot out of the sides. The manager is yelling 'Save the tea urns'. To add to it, monkeys are being blown through the

Water colour of beach and sea Ziamba, by Gunner Syd Carter

camp – they seek refuge in trucks, huts, etc. The hessian wall of the latrines shoots skywards revealing a line of straining figures on poles, hanging on like grim death to the straining bar. This wind was the famous North Africa Sirocco. The sand was like a whip lash on the skin. We shelter in the driving cabs with the windows up. Men are running after their kit. It's very dark – a monkey has bitten a gunner who tried to shoo him out of the back of his lorry. A fire has

NAAFI Store

broken out on distant hills, the sky-line is aflame. 'Has anyone phoned the fire brigade,' says Gunner Knott. 'The number's Bradford 999, it's next to a mortician's shop, I remember it caught fire one night and burnt all the stiffs, we were
in the cafe next door eating eggs and chips.'

By midnight it had blown itself out, the camp was in a
state. The NAAFI Sergeant was swearing. 'The monkeys
have eaten all the fuckin' buns.'

'They'll be dead in a week,' said Kidgell. He should know.
Next day I'm floating on the waters when Lt Budden calls
me from the shore. 'Come in Gunner number 954024, your
time is up.'

We were to pack up at once and report to L/Bdr Carter
for duty with the new Concert Party. There was a lot of
swearing from the lads. 'What a bloody thing to do on the
second day of our leave, they've got no respect for the dead.'

So back to Ain Abessa.

We returned at sunset. I wasn't pissed, but there, on a
trestle table was a seven foot hammer-headed shark.

Apparently the Major and Sgt 'Max' Muhleder set forth
from Ziama in a rubber boat and started fishing with gren-
ades. Suddenly a monster with eyes on oblique stalks shot up!
'Shark! Row for your life Sergeant!!!' He already was. They
got ashore, observed the monster still floating on top, and
returned. Chater Jack with a loaded pistol just stops himself
from saying 'Hands up'. The creature was dead, and here it
was, frying on a griddle and smelling delicious.

'Any chance of . . .'

'No, there fuckin' isn't,' says the Cook. 'Ask the Major.'

From inside the Major's tent I can hear straining of the
type one only hears in the Gents at Leicester Square.

'Major Chater Jack sir?'

'Milligan, can't you see I'm busy,' more heavy straining,
followed by a purple gasp. What *was* he doing??? Did he
wear a secret appliance? There follows a creaking unoiled
hinge sound, a gigantic heave, the unmistakable sound of a
cork from a bottle, a great exhaling of breath followed by a
pause, a swallowing sound then 'Ahhhhhh, now what is it
Milligan' it was a different man speaking.

'It's about your shark.'

'It hasn't bitten you has it?'

I bargained for a slice of the shark in exchange for my next fruit cake. To duplicate the taste of a hammer-head shark, boil old newspapers in Sloan's Liniment.

Suddenly came the Bad News. Major Chater Jack was being transferred to another regiment. Sadly he told us, 'I'm leaving you all. I don't want to, but it's promotion, and you know what that means.'

'More lolly,' says a voice.

Sgt Griffin chirps up, 'We're sorry to see you go, sir and we wish you the best of luck,' or something like that. It didn't matter, with his going the Battery was never the same again, we'd never been the same before, but now we were never going to be the same again.

The New Major

His name was Evan Jenkins. His physique? He didn't have one. The nearest description? Tut-an-Khamen with the bandages off. His neck measurement would be 11 inches, including shoulders. When a strong wind blew he had to hold his head to stop it from snapping off. His Adams apple stuck out like a third knee and when he swallowed, it disappeared down the front of his shirt and made him look pregnant. His arms must have been sent from Auschwitz; they were for all the world like two pieces of string with knots tied where the elbows were. His legs were like one of Gandhi's split in two. His eyes were so close together that to look left or right one of them appeared to cross the bridge of his nose. He had a pair of outsize ears which attracted flies. It got him the nickname Jumbo, but despite his comic appearance he was a real bastard; he had us taking our bootlaces out and ironing them so that they were 'nice and flat'. He made us use tooth-paste on our webbing to make it 'Nice and White' while our teeth went black. At night he'd sit in his tent and play 'Whistling Rufus' on a clarinet, and every morning he could be heard gargling with TCP then spitting it back into the bottle, the mean sod. He insisted on giving us cultural lectures. A

Sgt 'Griff' Griffin, one of the great characters of the Battery. He is here seen wearing either long shorts or short long trousers

'Jumbo' Jenkins

Sergeant, who shall remain nameless, said 'H'eyes front! now then, today the Major will be talking about' – (here he referred to a piece of paper) – 'Keats, and I don't suppose one of you higgerant bastards knows what a Keat is.'

Edgington and I decide to get our tent as far away from Jumbo as possible, so we found a distant Wadi over which we rigged up a canvas cover. Efforts to sabotage Jumbo were partially successful, we managed to impregnate the reed of his clarinet with soap, and he gave his batman hell over it. But it was by the Battery Cook Ronnie May that real revenge was wrought. May had collected dried goats shit, pounded it into a flour, mixed it with real flour and mashed potatoes, this mixture appeared on Jumbo's plate as rissoles, which he ate and asked for more, 'Now he really *is* full of shit,' said May.

The sky was blackening. It was going to rain.

Edgington.
Milligan tent
in Wadi.

'We could do with it,' says Edge.

'Do what with it?'

'For a start you can accept it.' The heavens opened and rain deluged down.

The Concise Oxford Dictionary says – WADI: Dried up water course. Filling quickly in rainy season.

We didn't have the Oxford Dictionary, but we found how remarkably accurate it was as we and our belongings floated out on a wall of water; all around were yells and shouts as tents were flattened.

'My bloody fags are down there,' said a drenched, mud reddened Edgington as he dove into the raging waters. Waist deep we ran among the flood grabbing kit and throwing it to high ground. It ceased as suddenly as it started.

'Why did it stop – 15 minutes more would have seen us off fucking Portsmouth.'

23 June 1943. With trees spaced its length, the road to Setif curved hither and thither – we were at a thither part.

'Are those Poplar trees?' said Kidgell.

'Very,' I said. We were bumping our way to the first rehearsal of the Concert Party.

We had been 'talent-spotted' the night of the French ENSA do by L/Bdr Bennett – he had told L/Bdr Carter, 'You must hear these lads.'

Outside the Municipal Theatre, there are posters advertising: GRAND CONCERT. 2 AGRA CONCERT PARTY

Gunner Edgington trying to save the tent during the storm

PRESENTS THE JOLLY ROGERS IN STAND EASY, IN AID OF THE ROYAL ARTILLERY BENEVOLENT FUND.

It's thirty two years since then, and so far no benevolence has reached us. The stage was alive with scruffy Gunners hanging up scenery; tuning the piano with a pair of pliers is the MD Gunner Sabin. Edgington confronts him.

'Are you a trained piano tuner?'

'No, that's why I'm in Africa.'

Ken Carter is on stage. 'Up here,' he said, and led us back stage. 'These are your dressing rooms.'

'We don't need 'em. We come ready dressed,' I said.

First Night of the Concert

Diary of Driver A. Fildes: July 28 1943. First night excited but OK: We heard that the French ENSA concert party had gone over a cliff on their way back to Algiers and had been in dock for three weeks, I prayed Mlle Villion's boobs were alright.

The Opening Night was attended by top brass and high ranking local French officials whose sole purpose in life was neither to laugh at, nor applaud anything. Back stage was alive with last minute crises.

Carter is hurrying in all directions, his hair falling out in handfuls, Lance Bombardier Reg Bennett is saying 'Fuck Show Business' over and over again. We four are being made

L/Bdr Reg Bennett who discovered our band during French Concert party

THE JOLLY ROGERS

Presenting

STAND EASY

A NEW REVUE

Producer:
 L/Bdr K. Carter

House Manager:
 Lt G. Broad

Compere:
 Captain G. Leahmann R.A.

Stage Manager:
 Lt W. J. Hoskins R.A.

Under the Direction of: Lt A. J. Chubb R.A.

---

1. The 'Agricans' will give you some old favourites.
2. Kiss the Blues Good-Bye
3. Foot – Steps – In   *Comic*
4. Swing – Trio   *Guitar, Clarinet, Drums*
5. Little Nell   *Capt. G. Leahmann*
6. Melody and Song   *Sgt P. Hulland*
7. Listening – In   *(In Town Tonight)*
8. String Serenade
9. Strip – Strip – Hoo-ray!!!   *'Fifi'*
10. Intermission
11. Red Hot and Blue   *D Battery Band*
12. I Spy
13. Accordionist Classique
14. Abdul – Hassan – Ohsonovitch   *Black Magic*
15. Melodious Memories   *Sgt Tucker Baritone*
16. Miss Prim *(School Marm)*   *Capt. G. Leahmann*
17. Let the People Sing.
18. In the Still of the Night.
19. Strike Up the Band.

Orchestra
under the direction of: L/Bdr Archer

Scenic Artists:
 L/Bdr Roberts
 L/Bdr Waller
 Gnr Carpenter, P.

Ensemble:
 L/Bdr Carter

Orchestration by:
 Gnr Sabin

Electrician:
 Cpl Straughan

Properties:
 Gnr W. Halls

–o–o–o–o–o–o–o–o–o–o–o–o–o–o–o–

up; blue eye shadow, rouge, lipstick, powder ... Kidgell looks up, 'Give us a kiss,' he said. I nearly did.

'It looks a good programme,' said Edgington, 'not a spoon player in it.'

Fildes comes in. 'The theatre's packed.'

'Well for Christ sake unpack it – we're due to start in 10 minutes,' I said.

A vast Gunner, in a vaster vest and shorts, is calling down the corridors 'Beginners please', and spitting out grape pips.

The pit band strikes up a tune which I recognised as 'The King' though I doubt if the Queen would; there follows a strangled version of the Royal Artillery March Past that suggests Gunners are cripples. The curtain rose, crashed down and rose again, the whole cast appear singing 'Kiss the Blues Goodbye'.

The show was away ...

Programme of Concert

When our turn came I announced 'Now! from the fabulous star studded 56 Heavy Regiment! the 19 Battery Jazz Quartet!' We started by my putting my trumpet through the curtains, beginning on a low C then dinging up to play 'Softly as in a Morning Sunrise' ... very loudly ... Then Kidgell sings 'Tangerine', we feature 'Snatch' on violin in 'Stardust', we round off with Nagasaki (Back in Naga-saki where the fellers chew tobaccy and the women wiggy-waggy-woo).

You can't *describe* a show, you have to *be* there at *that* time with *that* audience, *that's* what made it come alive. Come alive it did; troop audiences went into hysterics at the antics, and we got the sort of applause that would usually only be heard at a Promenade Concert.

A pencilled note at the foot of Part II Orders read: All ranks from now on will walk on their hands to keep their boots clean for parade.

The village of 'MacDonald'. We used to pass it on our way to Setif of an evening. Every wog – man or boy – we ever saw there, had red hair!!

2nd July 1943. After a week of success at Setif, the Concert party were to go on tour. 'I can't believe it,' said Edgington, 'I must rearrange my socks.'

'It's true,' I said, 'Bougie, Djelli, Phillipville and who knows – maybe Broadway!'

'All on the coast,' said Kidgell. 'We can swim every day!'

The Major calls me in and pep-talks me. 'Bombardier Milligan, you and 19 Battery band hold the honour of the Regiment when you are on the stage, I want you all to present a soldierly appearance, play in a smart military manner, keep your bugle straight, and salute at the finish. Try and play some stirring numbers, like "Whistling Rufus". Remember you are playing for your King and Country.'

'Yes sir, I will, and if ever I play a wrong note, I will immediately think of Hitler.'

'Good man Milligan.'

Mon. 3rd July '43. Dead on ten o'clock, three lorries containing the Concert Party set off for Bougie, some 60 kilometers away. We drove through the Kerrata Gorge, onto the Gulf of Bougie Coast Road heading West. It was scarifying. To our left were cliffs, and to our right a sheer 200 foot drop into the sea. I spotted dolphins pursuing a school of flying fish that kept breaking the surface and gliding up to fifty yards to escape; but the most exciting moment was when we were nearing Bougie. A huge Manta Ray broke the surface and came down with a colossal splash, it repeated this several times. 'His old woman must be after him,' says Snashall. We pass a company of 2/4 Hampshires marching like the clappers and covered in sweat, the only sympathy they got were cries of 'It'll be over by Christmas'. We drove in white sunlight, a light breeze coming from the coast. Bougie was a French Colonial town, now being used as a Naval base. The show was at the Municipal Theatre, modern-horror architecture, but cool inside. We have access to magnificent bathing, a curving bay shut off from the world by low hills, trees and Bougainvilleas which ran down to the beach, as we did. But wait! there on the beach are several WRENS, all brown and beautiful in bathing costumes. Why oh why, at the sight of a female does the male of the species automatically indulge in exhausting horse play? Wrestling, running, jumping, sparring, hitting, leaping acrobatics, even attempted murders? I mean by the time the Wrens noticed us, we were too shagged out to do anything about it. Bennett was different . . . he had started to dig about thirty yards away from the nearest Wren, he was actually trying to tunnel and come up beside her, he might have but for the great running feet of Gunner Carpenter who suddenly appeared to disappear into the ground, burying Gunner Bennett alive.

In the theatre props room, we had found a selection of plaster arms and legs with which we swam, holding them above the waves at arms' length.

Fifty yards from the shore was a rock shelf just below the surface, and, to the lads, I appeared to be walking on the water. 'There's only one other bloke done this,' I said and

Swimming holding prop legs under water .

100

awaited a thunderbolt from heaven. Instead, Edgington swims up and prepares one of his Captain Webb plunge dives, arms above head, palms touching, he is waiting for the Wrens to look. As they do I whip his drawers down, he lets out a high female scream, and, hands over his willy, falls into the water in the foetus position – that is foetus firstus. The Wrens have had enough, they leave. We shout after them in mock rage, 'You dirty little devils, we know why you joined the Navy,' says Kidgell, 'one day you'll come crawling back on your hands and knees.'

'She'll still be taller than you, short arse,' says Harry.

Ken Carter is lying half in, half out, of the Mediterranean, the waves lapping up his shorts. 'It's lovely,' he coos.

'From where I'm standin', it looks bloody 'orrible,' says Kidgell. There is a loud yell from Edgington who comes galloping from the sea. 'I bin stung,' he is shouting, and points to a red mark on his arm.

'It suits you,' I said.

It must have been the only jelly fish in a thousand miles but Edgington finds it. This was not the finish, in minutes three, it stung him again, surely a world's record. He got a stick and went thrashing at the sea in a foaming rage. 'I'll give it bloody jelly fish,' he was shouting when it stung him from behind for the third time.

We rehearsed the show in the cool of the evening, but Ken Carter was a stickler for perfection, so that it was midnight when we finished. We were all dog tired, and barked ourselves to sleep. We were billeted in a huge concrete school, on three floors, occupying what was a classroom with a running balcony overlooking the sea. At night the sea breezes afforded us a cool night's sleep. That's all we could afford.

Sunday, 4th July. Like all Catholics I asked God's forgiveness for missing Mass. Douggan, a devout RC confronted me. 'Did you miss Mass?'

'Not really,' I said.

'You know it's a mortal sin?'

'Yes, but I don't feel any different. I mean if they're going

The Rev. J. W. J. Steele, 1st Army Thanksgiving Service, blessing the microphone

to make sins into grades, then God should have made feelings to go with them, that is, if I commit a mortal sin, I should get a pain in the leg or something, otherwise it doesn't have any effect. Don't worry though, I'll do what all good lapsed Catholics do, relent on my death bed.'

'How do you know,' continued Douggan, putting his prayer book back in his big pack, 'that it's not your death bed you are laying on now?'

'I *don't* know, in any case, it's not mine, it's Kidgell's. He'll be very angry if I die on it, he's a Protestant.'

We spent the day on the beach, much the same as yesterday, we got very badly sun burnt. Kidgell's nose looked like a piece of shredded wheat, children screamed when they saw him.

'Cor, that sun's hot,' he said.

'Well you shouldn't touch it,' I said.

Edgington had found an old French brass baritone saxophone. He became obsessed with the idea that it was a sign from heaven and that he was to become 'a second Harry Carney'.* He took the instrument down to the beach and played it waist deep in water. He seemed quite happy, and after making a series of noises on it he announced, 'I've just played "I Got a gal in Kalamazoo".'

* Harry Carney: Duke Ellington's Baritone Sax player.

Col. Stirling, D.S.O., showing how to stop a vehicle when the brakes have failed

'You sure's she's not in Whipsnade?' said a surfacing head.

'I don't think you're going to become a second Harry Carney mate,' I said, 'a fifteenth or sixteenth maybe, but a second . . .'

When not in use, Edgington used most of the instrument as a clothes horse and the bell as an ash tray or spittoon. We rehearsed in the evening, and now had Gunner Douggan on double bass; this gave the band a wonderful life. He played a rock-steady two-in-a-bar while reminding me I was a Catholic. After rehearsal we took ourselves to an Arab café for dinner, and ordered eggs and chips. We stood on our balcony. It was midnight, and the moon-lit Mediterranean appeared like burnished black steel, from out to sea came the sound of heavy guns. 'Sounds like a Naval Engagement.'

'I hope they're both very happy,' I said.

Edgington blew a few smoke rings that remained suspended in the still air, slowly he passed his finger through one, bisecting it. Then we all went to bed for a night of traditional sleeping.

Navy Dance Bougie

6th July 1943. 'The Navy are holding a dance tomorrow, and they want you to play.'

'How much?' said my Jewish side.

'Sweet FA but all the booze you want.'

'OK.'

'Admiral Cunningham's coming.'

The 'do' was in the huge, school dining hall. The Navy, with a flair for such occasions, put up coloured bunting. We had finished our show by 9.00; the dance started at 10.00.

The top of the piano was lined with whiskey and gin.

'They're for you,' said a snotty.

'I told you we should have joined the bloody Navy,' said Kidgell.

By 10.30, the hall was packed with dancers, the heat of the African night was unforgettable, it was like a gigantic Sauna bath. We were getting through the grog. By 11.30 our KD's were black with sweat; still we drove the jazz along. Edgington went into a trance.

'What key are you in?'

'B♭.'

'I'd better come up ½ a tone and join you.'

We'd start a number but he'd have to wait a few bars to realize what it was. 'Go on,' he'd say, 'I'll catch you up.' The Wrens looked unbearably attractive in white uniforms and with tanned limbs. Oh the heat! the heat! the limbs! the limbs! By 1.30 I was stoned and making announcements like 'Schel-tage you're parlis for – ha! ha! ha! yes!'

'We're out of fags,' they're saying behind me.

'OK.' I approached Admiral Cunningham who was, despite the 3/4 tempo, dancing in 5/4.

'Excuse me sir,' I said.

'It's not an "Excuse me", soldier.'

'Excuse me sailor then, I wonder if you've got any fags.' He was about to have me flogged but, realizing I was the life and soul of the party, produced a packet of ships' Woodbines.

British officer in N. Africa explaining to a Chinaman that he is lost and should be in Chungking

British officer telling a civilian that he is nowhere near Surbiton

Someone had turned the light out to cool the place – shafts of moonlight lit up the interior.

By 2.00 several W R E N S had been molested, several men had been molested, all the booze had been drunk, red whiskey-filled faces staggered past, some with partners, sailors were dancing together. At 0230 hrs I've had enough because there was no more. Leaving Harry, Doug and Al still playing, I pushed through the sweating bodies up the stairs, along the long stone verandah to the classroom where we slept. I'd lost my mozzy net so I emptied my pallaisse and got inside. Later: THUD! GROAN! It had to be someone with a big head hitting a stone floor. Harry! of course! it was time for his accident, I got up, forgetting I was in a mattress and crashed to the floor. I pushed my feet through the bottom, and made for what was a huge drunken semi-conscious groaning figure – Sgt Hulland and Kidgell appeared, both naked. We stood round the slumped creature.

'It's Harry,' said Kidgell. 'He's shit himself.'

We dragged him by his lovely legs towards the shower at the end of the corridor.

'Orrgggg Arwagfff,' said the dragee. Standing him on his head, we slid the body from the trousers and reversed same for his shirt; we propped the dead shit-covered body under the shower and turned it on. He slept there all night. I heard a groaning thing approaching. It was 4.30 a.m.

'Let me in,' it said.

'There's no door,' I told it. It walked in, fell onto the bed, which splintered. We heard the head go thud for the second time, and he slept like an angel with a baby smile on his fizz.

There had been a time, when he was but three, his mother tucked him in and gave him his bottle. He'd come a long way since then.

The Morning After

My god! My head! Edgington's head! Fildes' head! Kidgell awoke me. 'Who am I?' he said. There's an inspection at 8.30 hours by Captain Leahmann, we had to 'stand by your beds', Edgington got as far as putting his vest on.

Then, exhausted, he just sat on his bed. Captain Leahmann said, 'What is it?'

'It's one of ours sir.'

'Why is it green?'

'It's something to do with an abnormal fluid intake.'

He stopped at Kidgell, unshaven, two unseeing red eyes staring over the blanket top.

'Does his mother know?' he said.

'Yes. It's Spazolikons sir.'

'Spazolikons?'

'Yes sir, only *he*, being short, has got them low down.'

This was all done straight faced.

'Very good Bombardier, carry on,' said Leahmann and left the room. I heard him burst into convulsive laughter outside.

Corporal tickling the feet of a German prisoner to try and make him see the joke

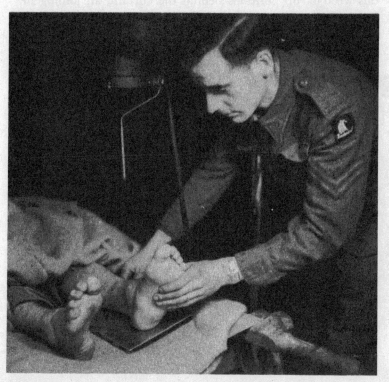

Alf Fildes Diary

Wed. 7 July 1943. Sorry to leave Bougie. 60 m to Djelli. Rehearsed in Glacier Cinema where we give show. Few civilians here. After short rehearsal we take a truck with band and posters to advertise show, funniest thing ever. Afternoon show fair, evening a wow! Standing room only. Crazy gang ad lib bits hilarious.

We packed up and set off to Djelli, 60 miles from Bougie. We drove along the spectacular Gulf of Bougie road, which hugged the coast. The scenery made mince-meat of tourists' valhallas like Nice, Costa Blanca and Blackpool. We were billeted in rooms back stage. The matinee was not too well booked, but the evening shows were a sell-out, and, of course, the show was forever improving, more and more gags being fed in. It was tending to become a 'Hellzapoppin'. In the show, Sergeant Hulland sang 'Jerusalem', and during this we took up positions behind the curtain, all joining in

Unknown artist's impression of the chaos during Ohsonovitchs' act in Stand Easy

harmony. Just for fun, Ernie Evans pulled the curtain to reveal the 'Holy Chorus' standing in underpants, towels, with some holding beer mugs.

'If that's the promised land, I don't want to know,' said Carter.

'I've just heard that the invasion of Sicily started at three this morning,' said Al Fildes in the interval.

At the end of the show we announced the news. The audience cheered. At last things were going *our* way.

Friday 9th July 1943. (Fildes' Diary.) Success again! Crazy Gang looking half nuts in insane selection of dressing up gear. Spike on Harry's shoulders, trombone case on head.

Edgington is 6 ft 3 – so with me on his shoulders it made 10ft 6, a trombone case on my head made us fifteen feet high. I am draped from waist downwards in a huge curtain that obscures Edgington – underneath is Kidgell holding a pole, with a boxing glove on, which shoots out hitting the bloke in front who is walking backwards spitting out 'pretend teeth'.

My Diary. Sunday 11th July. End of Tour. Packing up to return to unit.

We set off on a glorious sunny morning, loaded with local wines, cheese, fruits etc. Sprawled on top of the scenery is Edgington, his giant·saxophone wrapped in the Tricolore.

'Is it dead?' I said.

Driver Kidgell realizes it's twenty minutes since breakfast. 'Got any dates?' he asked hopefully.

'Yes,' I said. 'January the third 1895, and March the seventh 1923.'

Back at Ain Abessa mail is waiting. 'What's this? – Income Tax demand 1938-9?'

'Sir, it has been brought to our notice that in the year 1938/9 you received payments of money as a professional musician (see Sub. d. 3, para 9, section 76). Will you please remit immediately a list of payments received, dates and by whom the payments were made.' I send the following reply.

Date	Place	Band Leader	Tune	Payment £ s d
1st Jan. '38	Scrabble Rupture Appliances Ltd Annual Hernia Dance.	Tom Danger	Sweet Sue (2 chor.) Little Dutch Time Bomb Tick-Toch Boom.	0 10 1½ 0 14 3
May 6 '39	Dagenham District Ramblers Club	Eric Knotts.	Honeysuckle Rose.	3 6
Aug. 23 '39	Leeds Cat Crematorium Social.	Sir Henry Wood.	God Save the King.	gratis
June 6 '40	Dunkirk	Gen. Alexander.	The Retreat.	gratis
			Total £1 - 7 - 10½	

July 1943. The heat; 115 degrees! The African sky, lost in the reflected glare of the sun, appears like a distant white mist. It is empty save for one lone kite circling high. Work has stopped for the day, I'm on my bed re-reading old newspapers, there is a picture of the Queen inspecting runner beans on a bombed site allotment in Bethnal Green, another of Dorothy Paget watching her horse Straight Deal training for the Derby, and a hundred year-old villager in Tadworth ringing the bell for Victory in Tunisia. Would it be more newsworthy if we saw the Queen, on Straight Deal, eating the runner beans while Dorothy Paget pulls the 100 year old villager's Tadworth as he rings the bell for the start of the Derby, or the old man training 100 year old runner beans to climb up Dorothy Paget's legs as the Queen pulls a rope attached to Straight Deal as it trains for the Victory in Tunis, or the Queen pulling Runner Beans as 100 year old Dorothy Paget inspects an old villager's Victory bell for the Derby winner's legs?

A tent is speaking. 'I have a feeling, we should be home by Christmas.'

Christmas! I recalled my last one in England in 1942.

An OP on the coast of Bewhill. It was very cold, and I

General Montgomery wondering why he is surrounded by Chinese generals – as he neither drinks nor smokes

peered into the black of the English Channel – the bastards; they were only 20 miles away. Possibly, at that very moment Hitler was chasing Eva Braun with a sprig of holly. 'Kom mein darlink – let us do it under zer miseltoe – It is Christmas. I'll be Ping Crosby, dreaming on a white mattress.'

The telephone buzzed.

'O P,' I answered. There was stifled laughter from the other end, then a voice disguised as a ruptured Etonian said, 'Hell-o, who is that.'

'Gunner Milligan sir – who is that sir.'

'It's Lt Shagadog.' A burst of hysterical laughter then – click. It rang again. 'If that's Lt Shagadog he can piss off.'

'This is Captain Martin – have you been drinking Milligan?'

At which moment there was a terrific explosion from the mined field to my right – 'What was that, man?'

'I don't know sir.'

'Go and see what it was.' How do you go and look for a bang that's finished?

I ran down the hill – the grass in the mine field is on fire. A police constable on a bike said, ''Ello, wot's this then?'

I pointed. 'I think a mine went off.' He shone his torch.

A butcher's van arrived pulling a fire appliance – the Bexhill A R P Fire Brigade – a lot of little old men in pyjamas fell off it and started pulling a hose towards the fire.

'Put it out – 'urry – afore the bloody Germans see it –'

Just in time, we stop them walking into the mine field.

'We'll have to use high pressure,' said one who was doing nothing, and was therefore in charge, 'Where's the nearest fire hydrant?'

The policeman thought and said, 'Sea Road a mile away.'

'Hoses won't reach that far – ahh,' he held one finger in the air – 'Get the suction end in the sea lads.' Two little men throw their hose over the cliff. The tide's out. 'We must hurry,' shouted the leader, 'before it goes out.'

It started to rain, and the fire fizzled out. I returned to the

General Alexander showing troops how to play a concertina when you haven't got one

O P to the sound of a midget voice playing at high speed. My God! Captain Martin! I grabbed the phone.

'Where the hell have you been, I've missed six rounds.' Did he mean boxing or drinks? I explained the story.

'Be more careful in future,' was his final command.

Peace settled on the land.

'Is anyone in the Sentry Box.' It was an old lady.

'What is it, madam, this is a military area, civilians aren't allowed here?'

'I am a military,' she said, 'the WVS Reserve. Are those men on the cliff looking for my dog.'

'No.'

The dog!! THE DOG!!! of *course*!!!

'Do you live near the mine field,' I said.

'Right behind it . . . when the Germans come we'll have a lovely view of them going up . . . I've put gran's chair near the window.'

The news could have been broken to her less painfully. Next morning a policeman arrived, unwrapped a bit of newspaper revealing a tail, a leg and a collar.

'Is this your dog?' he said.

Tuesday 10th August 1943. My Diary. Since the Concert Party terminated, there had been unending demands from all Regiments for its return, so lucky lucky lucky, we start re-rehearsing. We are to do two more shows then fini. It's much the same as the old show except a few changes. Beryl Southby, a girl friend in Norwood, sent a new tune 'Happy Go Lucky' which we used for the finale.

Fri. 13 August 1943; Al Fildes' Diary: Show a wow: During this time all the Battery were away on a Calibration shoot out to sea near Ziama Rest Camp. From Ain Abessa we can see the gun flashes at night. Feels as if the war is coming close again. I don't like it.

Sat. 14 August. My Diary; Last night of show, Party on stage afterwards.

This was a send up with everyone doing everyone else's act. It went on until 2 a.m. and the wine flowed like water; towards the end of the evening it tasted like it.

Sun. 15 August 1943. I don't believe it! The whole Band are on guard, with me as guard commander! What a shambles we looked on parade. Edgington 6 foot 3, next to him Doug Kidgell 5 foot 6. Edgington had forgotten his gaiters and to do up his boot laces. The Battery returned during the guard mounting, and the cat-calls were too much to bear.

On August the 18th, our life of semi torpor and lotus eating came to an abrupt end. Suddenly, we were overwhelmed by a training programme that seemed intent on destroying us before the Germans did. It started with 20 mile route marches in full F S M O, through raging torrents, down thorn covered ravines, and up cactus covered cliffs. I left camp every morning a youth of 23, and came back at night looking like a seventy year old charlady. Even when you threw yourself on your bed, your legs went on marching.

'When this war's over I'm never going to stand up again.' said Kidgell.

Chinese defecating into a German tank just to show which side he's on

The programme reached its climax with a week on the Artillery ranges at Chateaux Dun in the most god-forsaken inhospitable countryside I'd ever seen. The ground was covered with loose hard rocks, so uneven, one sprained an ankle a day, and I only had two. We were issued with new No 19 and No 22 wireless sets which had to be carried on our backs. I watched as Major Jenkins led Edgington and Bombardier Trew up a sixty degree slope of crumbling rock, Edgington humping two batteries weighing a hundred pounds and Trew with a wireless on his back. In the broiling sun I don't know how they did it. I was link man between the OP and the Gun, both $\frac{1}{2}$ a mile away, I had to spend 48 hours on my own in utter loneliness without sight or sound of human habitation. At night I was terrified by strange sniffing sounds and for protection did that childlike thing, put my head under the blanket. Finally, on September the 4th it was all over. The Regiment left, leaving behind a small party of 'cleaner uppers', of which I was put in charge. We had to collect all the rubbish and bury it. We took our time. By the evening we'd finished and drove back.

It was a warm, dark night, the air caressing, the palm trees appear as velvet cut outs, the meadows of heaven are chorusing stars. The glow of Edgington's cigarette bounced in the dark corner of the lorry. No-one spoke, which was rare for us. We really *were* shagged out. It's 2100 hrs, the lorry gradually slowed to a halt. 'Ain Abessa centre of the Universe,' said Driver Shipman. 'All change.' Did he mean underwear? Edgington jumped down from the tail board like a lad of twenty and hit the ground like a man of ninety. That night we slept like dead men. Even a thunder storm in the night didn't wake us.

Sept. 5th 1943. Battery Diary: All light vehicles left for Phillipville staging at Ain Milia.

This means we lost Al Fildes. We said goodbye, 'see you somewhere some time'. He gave us a thumbs up and a smile as he drove off with the convoy. It was all happening. We were given no rest. Intensive signal training. We had to learn new Signalling Codes, we had to a opt the American phonetics. A used to be Ack, it was now Able, B used to be Beer, it was now Baker and so on. We were told to replace all our old kit, for most of us that meant everything, our K D's were so threadbare the Arabs refused to steal them, my underwear on a line looked like distress signals from shipwrecked tramps.

8th September 1943. Italy have surrendered!

9th September 1943. 5th Army lands at Salerno; there is heavy fighting. 8th Army lands in the South unopposed.

The days that followed were all focused on the wireless news about Salerno, it was obvious that it was pretty tricky

Condition of L/Bdr Milligan's kit at end of Tunis Campaign

An Italian soldier, having been captured, takes up the culinary art in hopes of opening a Trattoria in London

going, with the 8th Army hurrying up the coast to link up with the 5th.

On the 13th of September Alexander signalled Churchill, 'I consider situation critical,' of course I didn't know that at the time, no, I had to buy Alexander's Biography in 1973 to find out and by then it was too late for me to worry. It was a near thing! All our vehicles are being waterproofed, it looks like a beach landing.

'Oh yes, waterproof the bloody vehicles, what about us?' says Gunner White, 'it doesn't matter if we drown.'

10th September 1943. Loading party return from Phillipville, where they have been loading vehicles onto cargo ships, we're all puzzled, if we were waterproofing vehicles why are they on cargo ships????

'Somewhere, Harry,' I said, 'there is a lunatic. Every day

he's taken from Colney Hatch, locked in a room with a phone at the War Office, he phones through a series of orders and these are transmitted directly to us.'

Edgington nodded his head and laughed. 'It's something like that,' he said.

Now dear reader, a blank appears in my memory, all there is in my diary is the word PISSED. This happened between Sept. 10th and the 11th. But I recall arriving back in a lorry with Edgington to Ain Abessa to discover the Camp deserted.

'They've deserted without us,' said Edgington jumping down.

'Wait! an oil lamp glows in yon Nissen hut,' I said.

A figure filled the doorway. It was Bdr Fuller. 'Where's everybody?' I said.

'They've gone to secret destination 397,' says Fuller donning his crash helmet.

He gave us 15 minutes to pack any gear we had left in the Nissen hut. We were all a bit dazed by the change of events, here we were looking forward to a good night's sleep, and now we were off to somewhere.

'This is an outrage,' said Edgington as he strained, lifted and hurled his kit onto the lorry.

'It's also an inrage,' I said, carefully mixing my kit with his.

'We've got to catch up with the main convoy,' said Fuller, 'they're 10 hours ahead.'

'Australia's only 8.'

'Let's chase that – it's nearer.'

'Hurry up,' shouts Fuller, 'we're keeping Adolf waiting.'

'Fuck 'im,' said a voice under some strain.

'Right away.' Edgington slams the tailboard, and bangs on the side.

Off we drive in exactly the same direction from which we had come. With a rolled blanket for a pillow, I fell into a deep sleep. I awoke with a start, we appeared to be driving over a field of corrugated iron, the vibrations moved us about like chess pieces. Edgington, still asleep, passed me on his way to the tailboard, the quality of the vibrations

118

Churchill during a lull in the fighting deciding which US General to fire next

changed and Edgington passed me again. Through the back of the lorry I saw a late moon, it bounced like a ping pong ball as the lorry jolted. Edgington was going towards the tailboard again, he was awake. 'Wot's the time?' he yawned. I held up my wrist-watch waiting for a shaft of moonlight.

'Well . . . what's the time?'

'I'm waiting for the moon.'

'You can tell the time by the moon?'

'It's exactly 0400.'

'What is?'

'The moon.'

We slept fitfully on, at intervals we heard trucks going the other way. While we slept the Anglo American 5th Army were locked in a grim slaughtering battle. It was touch and go, with Kesselring throwing everything in to hurl the Allies back into the sea. If he did, it would be a devastating blow, especially for Churchill who conceived the idea of attacking the soft underbelly of Europe, though troops in the beach head would be saying, 'soft underbelly, my arse!'

Sept. 11/12 1943. My Diary. Caught up with main convoy at 0500 hrs just outside Ain Milia. Breakfast amid olive groves. Bought delicious green grapes in village. Convoy is waiting for a lost truck to turn up, by midday no sign of it, so we all push on again:

I spent the whole day asleep in back of truck only waking for food. By nightfall we had arrived at Ghardimaou, it was so dark I've no idea what the place looked like. I went on sleeping as fast as I could so we could get there quicker, I slept all night and only awoke when Gunner Edgington said ''Ere Rip Van Watsit' and gave me a cup of tea.

We walked to the Wireless Truck for the 7 o'clock news about Salerno. The announcer was saying, 'Three attacks by Panzers were thrown back in the night.' It all sounds dodgy.

A huge formation of Baltimore Bombers passed overhead in the direction of Sicily. 'That ought to cheer the lads up,' said Ben Wenham. 'If they're American, they're as likely to drop the bloody lot on *us*,' said White.

Drivers are warming up their engines, they are dispersed among the olive trees, affording ideal camouflage for the vehicles which are painted black and green.

'Prepare to move!' The order rings through the camp. Diesel fumes turn the air blue, gradually the convoy pulls onto the 'road', the leader raises his hand, drops it, and we pull away. This was a slow convoy pulling heavy guns, the speed averaged thirty miles an hour. We had crossed the border into Tunisia and were passing familiar battle grounds where the skeletons of German tanks lay rusting. In the fields, amid grazing sheep, Arabs are re-working the land, ploughing round the shell holes. We passed acres of cork trees and groves of eucalyptus trees, it all seemed so peaceful, yet here we were, obviously headed for Salerno and bloody hell! We passed Sidi Nsir where the gallant 155 Battery had made their stand against General Lang's 10th Panzer and Mark VI Tanks of 501 Heavy Tank Bn17, the guns were fought to the muzzle, only 9 Gunners survived but they put paid to the German advance.

Churchill listening as troops of the 1st Army address him

Sept. 13th 1943. We have travelled 500 miles in three days, or is it three miles in 500 days? Whatever, it was bloody rough and dusty, the ending jolting and bumping, numbing mind and body alike. Everywhere now are massive American Camps and Dumps, mile after mile of shells and supplies, tanks and vehicles. Batallions of marching infantry are everywhere; our destination was a mile outside Bizerta, near the great salt Lac de Bizerta, a vast camp called Houston and Texas. There seemed to be absolutely no organization so we presumed it was ours. The country was a mixture of the flat and the hilly, covered in brown tussock grass all flattened by thousands of vehicle tracks. We put our bivvies anywhere we liked, and waited.

'Wot's on then?' inquires Chalky White.

'I'm doing military waiting.'

'Military waiting?'

'Yes, definitely military waiting.'

'Wot for?'

'That is something I don't know, all I know is that I am waiting in military, and by your appearance, you are also military waiting.'

'You know, I've been walking around here for an hour, and I didn't know what I was doing and all the time I was military waiting.'

Edgington, Devine and Tume are approaching with military waiting.

'Got any fags?' was the query, I distributed a packet of Passing Clouds my parents had sent me. I had up till now refrained from using them, as they had been packed in a parcel with bars of soap. Smoking them was exactly like chewing a bar of Lifebuoy, however they smoked them in complete agony, but such is the power of nicotine that Edgington bought the whole packet. Thereafter it was easy to tell when he'd been smoking one as he went grey and his spit turned to bubbles. We found a huge NAAFI in a marquee. There was a brand new upright piano, so we gave the lads a session of Jazz, until a spoon player appeared.

Sept. 14. Thank God! Pay Parade! What's this? It's in lire? So it is Italy for sure. We are given a small booklet. Customs and language of Italy.

'It says the Italians are very jealous of their women, and in the South they are usually chaperoned . . .'

'Wot's chaperoned.'

'Means they orlways got someone wiv 'em.'

'OH? What 'appens if you want to 'ave it away wiv her.'

'Well the chaperon 'as to be done as well, otherwise they won't let you do it at all.'

The daily routine; Morning Parade with small Arms.

Maintenance and training.
Lunch.
Afternoon off.

The afternoon was spent doing laundry and writing letters in the NAAFI. Usually a lorry went down to a great surf beach at Cap Blanc just outside Bizerta, which was crowded with American troops. The sea here has huge breakers and great fun was had by diving into them, or coming in surfboard style.

From the 15th to the 20th we passed the time as best we could, and it wasn't good enough. Apparently we were waiting for landing craft from Salerno; they had stayed longer than anticipated, as at one stage it seemed as though they would have to evacuate the beach-head. We played football games that went on for hours with sides of up to 50, scores like 63 goals to 98 were not uncommon. Our MO described the camp as the only lunatic asylum run by the inmates. I wrote home to my brother

Dear Hairy,

Don't ask me what is happening. It's whispered that the war is over and no-one has the nerve to tell us. The American troops don't know what we are, they drive past in Cadillacs, throw us sweets and ask where our sisters are. We play 500 a side football, it's the only way one can get a game. The NAAFI queue is nine miles long, the men at the front are from World War One. Our major wants us to invade Italy so he can see Vesuvius 'before it goes out'. He is a brilliant soldier and can almost dress himself. It's a very trying time. Try it. Love to Mum and Dad.

Ever loving Brother known as 954024

Sept. 21st 1943. This evening we collected the Camp Rubbish and lit a bonfire. We gathered around and sang (to the tune of Alouette)

Balls to Jumbo
Balls to Jumbo Jenkins

Among those singing loudest is Captain Bentley, the Regimental Chaplain.

We sat and watched as the embers finally died, then we retired to our tents. I lit my little oil lamp and read 'The Persians' by Aeschylus. I'd never been a scholar as such but had a voracious appetite for knowledge and wished to know what the Golden Age of Greece was like, and to learn about its inheritors the Romans; so my father sent me many books on the subject, though my choice baffled him, for he was reading Wild Bill Hickock, Buffalo Bill and Dead Wood Dick, and I think he still is.

22 September 1943: Battery Diary: First Party embarked (Part of HQ, 17 and 19 Batteries).
In terms of the physical it started when a crowd of our officers started to run at high speed in all directions crashing into one another and finally disappearing into the HQ Tent, shoe sides bulged outwards with the combustion of Commissioned Ranks within. Suddenly the tent flaps burst open, and out thunder the officers. Lt Pride says, 'We're off lads, as usual it should all have been done yesterday,' a great scramble ensues, and by ten o'clock we are on the way to

HMS Boxer the LST that took us to Salerno

whatever it was we were on the way to, which turns out to be Bizerta Docks. Some Hundred LST are lined up, jaws open, waiting to devour us. Through the stifling day, in that peculiar muddled British style, we load our vehicles onto the HMS Boxer, we watch her sink lower and lower in the water, as hour after hour we pile our gear aboard.

'There's no bunks, sleep wherever you can,' said Lt Pride.

We are issued with seasick pills. I never suffer from this so I threw them over the side where fish ate them and were immediately sick.

'It's all very exciting,' says Kidgell. 'Wonder what they're going to do with us.'

'First make us sea sick, and when we are vomiting at our limit, land us on a beach in Italy under shell fire.'

The ramp is being winched up. ''Ello, we're off then,' the engines throb into 'Hard Astern', we hear the ring of the ship's telegraph. We pull away from the jetty, we are all lining the railing. It's six o'clock as we pull into the middle of Lac de Bizerta.

'Well,' says Doug Kidgell, rubbing his hands with excitement, 'we're off at last,' whereupon we drop anchor.

'You were saying?' I said.

There's a cool breeze from the sea. 'Grub up,' we all troop down to the galley where containers of hot stew are opened and doled out with a mug of ship's cocoa.

'Like a fag?' A sailor, short and squat, holds out a fifty tin of ships' Woodbines, in those days a luxury. 'Ta,' I said with a certain amount of surprise.

'Take a handful,' he said. 'This is a trap,' I thought.

'You're not queer are you,' I said.

His name was Eddie Hackshaw. As darkness fell there was a feeling of frustration on board, so I got out me bugle and, down on the mess deck, blew some tunes. Eddie Hackshaw was so pleased he gave me a silver Arab ring.

'It will bring you good luck,' he forecast.

'Good luck?' I said. 'What's that.'

He wangled an extra mug of cocoa for me before we all settled for the night. Doug Kidgell and I slept on top of his

Scammell. It was incredibly quiet. We could hear the lap of waves against the ship.

As I lay, stretched out on top of the huge Scammell lorry, believing I would surely die at Salerno, I started to cogitate on my Will, the last one I had made out was when I was due to get killed in the North African landings, however, we had arrived too late. My most expensive possession was my trumpet, I wanted that buried with me in case I am buried alive, I could blow a few bars and they would dig me up again. Second most expensive item, twenty Wills Woodbines in an old tobacco tin. Then there were the women ... 'Listen to this Kidgell – I want you to be a witness, it is my last Will and Testament.'

'You making it out on top of a lorry?' he said in disgust.

'No better place – listen, my women – I leave Ivy Chandler and three Woodbines to Gunner Chalky White. I leave Kay of Herstmonceux to Gunner Devine, I leave Betty Ormsman and one Woodbine to Gunner Kidgell.'

'Is that the one with the big boobs?'

'Yer.'

'Smashing ... but only one Woodbine?'

'That's all you'll have time for with her! ... Now to Gunner "Plunger" Bailey, I leave Shirley Wright, Mrs Eileen Leech and Molly Parkinson.'

Gunner Edgington attempting to smuggle Gunner Milligan out of Africa in a NAAFI tea chest

'That's not enough for 'im.'

'It'll have to do . . . this is an emergency . . . Now to my mother, I leave my brother, to my father I leave my mother.'

'Wot you going to leave your brother?'

'I'm going to leave him alone . . .'

Those were the last thoughts as I dropped into a sleep that would terminate in Volume IV . . . what time will Bombardier Milligan arise, what will be his first words to the dawn . . .? Read all about it in Volume IV, order your copy to-day. I need a reason to start writing it.

'I wonder why we're waiting?' I said as I threw my stub-end over the side.

'We're waiting for the tide,' says Kidgell.

'That's the best news I've had.'

'Why?'

'The Med's tideless.'

He just wanted a decent book to read ...

Not too much to ask, is it? It was in 1935 when Allen Lane, Managing Director of Bodley Head Publishers, stood on a platform at Exeter railway station looking for something good to read on his journey back to London. His choice was limited to popular magazines and poor-quality paperbacks – the same choice faced every day by the vast majority of readers, few of whom could afford hardbacks. Lane's disappointment and subsequent anger at the range of books generally available led him to found a company – and change the world.

'We believed in the existence in this country of a vast reading public for intelligent books at a low price, and staked everything on it'
Sir Allen Lane, 1902–1970, founder of Penguin Books

The quality paperback had arrived – and not just in bookshops. Lane was adamant that his Penguins should appear in chain stores and tobacconists, and should cost no more than a packet of cigarettes.

Reading habits (and cigarette prices) have changed since 1935, but Penguin still believes in publishing the best books for everybody to enjoy. We still believe that good design costs no more than bad design, and we still believe that quality books published passionately and responsibly make the world a better place.

So wherever you see the little bird – whether it's on a piece of prize-winning literary fiction or a celebrity autobiography, political tour de force or historical masterpiece, a serial-killer thriller, reference book, world classic or a piece of pure escapism – you can bet that it represents the very best that the genre has to offer.

Whatever you like to read – trust Penguin.